You shouldn't have
gone to so much
trouble, darling

Best wishes from

Jo Seagar

JO SEAGAR'S

You shouldn't have gone to so much trouble, darling

PHOTOGRAPHY BY
JOHN DALEY

RANDOM
HOUSE
NEW ZEALAND LTD

ACKNOWLEDGEMENTS

My sincere appreciation and thanks to my photographer and dear friend John Daley. Special thanks to Juliet Rogers, Harriet Allan and Gillian Kootstra, Random House for their enthusiasm, encouragement, editorial help and patience. To Penny Bieder for cleverly decoding and editing my scribbles. To Anne Stuart for exceptional secretarial skills. To John and Yo Robinson, Inverness Estate for friendship and lending me their bath. To supernanny Niki Stirling for keeping the home fires burning and the chookies fed. To Jo Ashton and Bridget Bannister for all your help. To Maree O'Neill (makeup and stylist) for helping me to look 'glam' on the cover. And especially to my mother Fay, my husband Ross, and my children Kate and Guy for being good while I got on with this!

Random House New Zealand Ltd
(An imprint of the Random House Group)

18 Poland Road
Glenfield
Auckland 10
NEW ZEALAND

Sydney   New York   Toronto
London   Auckland   Johannesburg
and agencies throughout the world

First published 1997
Reprinted 1998 (twice)
© 1997 Jo Seagar
The moral rights of the Author have been asserted.

Photography (including cover) by John Daley
Wheatsheaf logo by Bridget Wellwood

Printed in Hong Kong, CHINA.
ISBN 1 86941 330 X

CONTENTS

Dedicated to my dear father Marty who died earlier this year
— one of the great party boys from way back whose warmth of welcome and hospitality
is legendary.

INTRODUCTION

*If you want to cook food for your guests that
tastes wonderful and looks spectacular – food that appears as
if you have spent hours preparing, but in fact was dazzlingly
simple to put together, then read on
.... this is the book for you.*

I think there's a new rebellion out there against the too long-accepted model of toiling over a hot stove. Don't get me wrong. I love to cook, but when faced with a sack of onions that needs to be peeled and sliced I'm quite ready to spread my love around.

We all need to know how to cut corners with tips on what freezes and what doesn't. What packaged foods can be improved upon, what brands do we buy, and most important of all, how do we cover all traces of the most outrageous cheating? (I don't quite go as far as transferring lowly wine to lordly bottles, but help is at hand.)

If you have heaps of taste and style but only a little time, entertaining can be a daunting prospect. It's very natural to worry about managing guests and orchestrating a fabulous dinner party but no longer is it the sole measure of your competency and worth. Just because a meal is incredibly complicated to cook doesn't necessarily mean it's going to be a fantastic, successful evening.

The impulse to entertain with grace and style never changes but luckily for us styles themselves do change and so does the definition of grace. Social dictates about the order and number of courses — whether the cheese knives go on the left or right and which finger bowls to use — have thankfully all gone out the window now, and all that stuff is passé.

Today the right ways to do things far outnumber the wrong, which is very handy for me because there seems to be a natural law that operates on days when I am planning to entertain. Invariably a late afternoon crisis crops up at the office, or an urgent dash to the local Accident and Emergency Department with child in tow, sporting a riding-or rugby-induced suspected broken arm. I find my biggest help with entertaining is the psychological weapon of understanding that it really is OK to be yourself. In fact, it is highly desirable.

I find that one's life experience, and the ability to accept perfection as the goal rather than a necessity, is an excellent antidote to culinary stress and tension. You don't want to find you have spent more time on all the party trivia — like who's sitting where, and have you got out the butter knife — than on the real job of being focused on your guests.

I am writing this book for harassed but discerning cooks who like to serve impressive dishes to their friends but are not actually willing to lay down their lives for the cause.

This book is not for beginners who need clear instructions on how to turn on the oven, make a white sauce, or fit the lid to the food processor (mind you, that can be darn tricky at times). I've written it for people who are perfectly competent, traditional cooks, when they want to be. I hope it will be an invaluable source for those who feel panic at the prospect of entertaining. It's intended for busy people who want to enjoy their dinner parties and not end the evening feeling physical and nervous wrecks.

We all need inspiration and new ideas of dishes to serve. So often people get stuck on menu number three — that apricot chicken thing and the same old never-fail pud which is all very well but a bit boring for guests who come around again more than three times.

My recipes are simple to follow with clear instructions and none of that complicated cookbook jargon. I generally mix things all in the one bowl, and for measurements I have used cups and spoons. Who knows what 7 grams of dried yeast is, or 324 grams of flour? As for a gill being a quarter pint, who cares? I know what a G & T is and I would much rather be drinking one with my friends in the living room than going solo out in the kitchen wrestling with a set of scales, flambéeing, or reducing a dodgy sauce. I'm

too busy for recipes that start with 'take 16 cups of homemade chicken stock'. Sure, I know how to make it, but let's get real!

There are no recipes in here where you have to hand whisk, parboil, chine bones, infuse, blanch, baste or any of that sweating of vegetables or peeling of mushrooms. Yes, I have included recipes for quite tricky things like bread-making but, hey! mine uses a can of beer instead of yeast or focaccia bread that you make in a food processor, so none of that icky sticky dough-kneading, and as for that 'over-achiever stuff' about grinding your own flour, forget it!

I love the praise at dinner parties. I am a perfectionist in that I want to serve stylish, memorable meals that they'll be talking about for months; but the praise should be because I am such a clever cheat and not because I have slogged my guts out in the kitchen all day and now, come evening, I'm a physical wreck.

People say 'My, you have been busy' and yes, I smile, I sure have been, but not shredding, blending and hand grating. I have been busy with two small children, writing a book, working on a magazine story, running a farm, doing my stint as parent help, or at a PTA meeting and after lunch of course there have been my helicopter flying lessons!

Don't begrudge yourself all the help you can get in the form of dishwashers and microwaves. Kitchen gadgets like food processors and icecream machines are not extravagant luxury items. I am sure even the great doyenne herself, Mrs Beaton, would have approved. Mind you, things have changed somewhat since she wrote her classic book *Everyday Cooking and Housekeeping*, full of invaluable little tips like 'Always pay the butler more than the acceptable going rate' and 'Upon entering the kitchen invariably say Good Morning, cook.' Well that's a great lot of advice for busy people like you and me. We need all the practical help we can get in cutting corners and quelling anxiety, so treat your kitchen gizmos, blenders, waste disposal units and pasta machines as the entire cast of *Upstairs and Downstairs*.

You need to arm yourself with heaps of my clever little helpful hints. For example, when a guest asks you for the recipe as you are stuffing the last incriminating remains of the packaging into the trash can, say: 'Sure! Remind me before you leave and I'll fax it to you,' or better still, ask them what their e-mail address is, and hopefully the request will be lost in the joys of modern technology conversation that follows.

Absolutely guard against modesty. It's so unbecoming in a cook. Never say how easy it was, and never apologise, the 'if only I had fresh tamarind or a bay tree in the herb garden' type of thing. If something gets a trifle burnt just bring it to the table and say 'I don't think I would bother with that final chargrilling step of the recipe, I don't think it adds much to the dish!'

First impressions are so important. It's too late after serving 'ho-hum' nibbles, entrées, mains and salad to then try to 'knock 'em dead' with a spectacular pud. You have to stun them right from the first instance. Make it look like trouble was taken — soft lighting, I always use candles — and lovely fresh flowers. If I have time it's an over-the-top 'Queen Mother fluff' arrangement, or if I'm in a mad rush it's my interpretation of Japanese modern, ie two branches of budding pussywillow and a couple of 'glad the impalers' jammed in a vase.

Have a drinks tray ready, all beautifully set out, with masses of ice, champagne and scrumptious nibbles. Little bites of 'drop dead impressive' smoked salmon and caviar (for caviar read lump fish roe; and remember, the more you use the less they think it's real, so be a bit of a meanie with it).

Read on for tips on how to stretch a meal with style — crisp green salads, gorgeous, fresh fruit, easy puds and country breads. Cook complicated-shaped pasta. Anyone can cook spaghetti and macaroni but somehow you get far more brownie points for tackling tortellini. My advice for when guests invariably ask what they can bring to dinner is, don't go onto autopilot and say 'bring nothing'. Whenever I experiment with democracy in dinner party entertaining it never works. Instead I say 'Why don't you bring the cheese and this is the one I think you should buy.'

While we can't obliterate what we have learnt about health and diet, we can at least choose to liberate ourselves from it now and then. I'm the first to admit some of my recipes may be so 'soulful' that their love content far outweighs their fat content. My cooking and eating and entertaining beliefs are based on moderation not deprivation. (I understand this principle on an intellectual level but sometimes lose it on the emotional side.) However, this is not a low fat, low salt, low taste epistle nor is it the 'cheapo' how to feed a family of ten on a pound of mince kind of book. It's about maximum effect for minimum effort entertaining, and how to produce impressive, delicious food when you feel it's worth investing a little extra money when you don't have the luxury of extra time.

Ross and I entertain a lot. We also entertain impulsively, inviting friends for a drink and then asking them to stay on for the weekend. It's important to have the larder and freezer in a state of constant readiness. Special occasions are always celebrated around the dining table in our family. Nostalgia colours many of the pleasures we get from cooking and eating. Our memories of taste and enjoyment come heavily laden with memories of when, where and with whom we ate a particular food or dish, so make your dinner parties really memorable — and that's not always just about the food!

Cooking for friends is like a generous gift offered to the people you care about the most. Angst is the cook's worst enemy, therefore get rid of it and remember the essential main ingredient is love for those you are cooking for. So relax, enjoy and now go get into that kitchen and rattle those pots and pans!

NIBBLES

PARMESAN WAFER BISCUITS

Makes about 12

These delicious and delicate little melted cheese biscuits can be served warm or at room temperature. They stay translucent and crisp. You can use them as a drinks nibble or to garnish salads and entrées.

1 cup grated parmesan cheese
optional: cumin, caraway, celery or sesame seeds or
freshly ground black pepper
clarified butter for frying

Melt approximately 1 teaspoon of butter in non-stick frypan over medium/low heat. Sprinkle about a tablespoon of parmesan cheese into the pan spreading it out to the size of a crumpet or pikelet. Sprinkle with 1/2 teaspoon of seeds or a good grind of black pepper and press this down with a spatula. Let the cheese melt slowly and begin to colour and harden. Flip over, adding a little extra butter to the pan if required. They should take a couple of minutes each side. Drain on paper towels.

BACON OR ANCHOVY WHEELS

Makes about 30 wheels

2 sheets frozen flaky puff pastry, thawed
10 rashers rindless streaky bacon (or 10-12 anchovy fillets)
garlic salt

Join the 2 sheets of pastry by wetting the edge and crimping together with a fork. Roll out the pastry even thinner until it measures roughly 60 x 30 cm. Lay the streaky bacon across the pastry, sprinkle generously with garlic salt and roll up tightly, like a spring roll. Seal the end by wetting with water and crimping with a fork. Cut into approximately 1 cm thick slices and place on an oiled baking tray. Bake at 200°C for about 10 minutes then turn over and bake another 4–5 minutes until crispy and well puffed. Cool slightly on a wire rack and serve immediately. These can be made ahead of time, frozen and reheated.

To make anchovy versions, replace the bacon rashers with 10–12 mashed anchovy fillets which you spread over the pastry like butter. Leave out the garlic salt as the anchovies are quite salty, but add a sprinkle of pepper. Roll up and cook as above.

CRISPY CHEESE-WRAPPED OLIVE BALLS

Makes about 25

1/2 cup tasty cheese, grated
50 grams butter, softened
1 cup flour
pinch cayenne pepper
pinch salt
20-25 medium size stuffed green olives

Mix the cheese, butter, flour and pepper together in a food processor until smooth.

Enclose each olive in approximately a teaspoonful of pastry, pinching it around the olive to completely seal. Chill for at least 20 minutes. Bake on a flat oven sheet at 200°C for approximately 15 minutes until lightly golden brown. Cool on wire racks.

SWEET CHILLI, BASIL & CHEDDAR QUESADILLAS

Serves 4

1 cup cheddar cheese, grated
4 flour tortillas
2 teaspoons Thai sweet chilli sauce
6-8 large fresh basil leaves

Spread 2 flour tortillas with sweet chilli sauce (like spreading jam), about a teaspoon on each. Sprinkle with grated cheese and basil leaves. Then lay on the top tortillas.

In a non-stick frypan just lightly oiled or sprayed with olive oil, cook tortillas over medium heat for 2-3 minutes or until lightly golden brown and the cheese has melted. Turn once and cook other side. Slide out onto a board and cook second quesadilla.

Cut quesadillas into wedges (I find kitchen scissors best) and stack on a serving plate.

ONION MARMALADE IN TINY PASTRY CASES

Pastry Cases
sheets of frozen, pre-rolled savoury pastry
(I find Ernest Adams very good)

With a round cookie cutter, approximately 6 cm diameter, stamp out circles of pastry (you should get 16 per sheet) then press into the base of mini muffin tins. Jam an identical tin into the pastry-lined tin and bake upside down in a coolish oven, about 130°C for 8–10 minutes. Carefully remove the top tin and continue to bake pastry cases until just coloured and dry. Cool on a wire rack and store in an airtight container.

Onion marmalade is wonderful as a garnish on fingers of toast with pâté or as a sauce for steak, either on its own or stirred through sour cream.

Onion Marmalade
4 large Pacific Sweet onions (if substituting another variety of onion add
a little sugar to increase sweetness, approx. a teaspoonful per onion)
1 cup beef stock
2–3 tablespoons prepared grainy mustard
1/4 cup balsamic vinegar

Roughly chop onions and place in a large frypan with the beef stock. Add the sugar (if not using Pacific Sweet variety of onion). Gently simmer until the stock is evaporated and the onion is golden and caramelised, approximately 20–25 minutes. If the stock evaporates too quickly add a little water until you achieve the caramel colour. The Pacific sweet onions do caramelise brilliantly but other types of onion take a little longer and you may need to cheat with a tiny dash of gravy browning if they remain too pale. Stir in the mustard and balsamic vinegar and cool. This will keep in a small covered container in the fridge for weeks.

To serve, place a teaspoon of sour cream in the base of each pastry case and top with a teaspoon of onion marmalade (it is good to leave a little bit of the sour cream showing). Garnish with a tiny sprig of fresh herb, parsley or dill.

Steps for making tiny pastry cases, filled with onion marmalade

MANGO CHUTNEY SPREAD

Serve in pastry cases or spread on crostini or crackers.

250 gram tub of spreadable cream cheese (approx. 1 large cup)
150 gram tub of sour cream (approx. 3/4 cup)
4 tablespoons of mango (or similar good flavoured) chutney
3 tablespoons chopped parsley

Mix all ingredients together in a small bowl with a fork until smooth and well blended. Chill covered until required. Can be prepared a day or two in advance.

SMOKED SALMON & CAVIAR SPREAD

Serve in pastry cases or spread on crostini or crackers.

250 gram tub of spreadable cream cheese (1 large cup)
100 grams approx. (1/2 cup) smoked salmon pieces or off-cuts, chopped
2–3 teaspoons red lumpfish roe (caviar)
3 tablespoons chopped parsley
1/2 cup tiny cooked shrimp
1 teaspoon lemon pepper seasoning
2 teaspoons prepared horseradish sauce

Mix all ingredients together in a small bowl with a fork until smooth and well blended. Chill covered until required. Can be prepared a day or two in advance.

BABY SAVOURY PIKELETS

Makes about 25

1/2 teaspoon salt
1 teaspoon soda
1 cup milk
2 eggs
2 cups flour
2 teaspoons cream of tartar
1 tablespoon finely chopped parsley

Well-risen 'fat' little pikelets are topped with cream cheese and smoked salmon, sliced avocado, chargrilled pepper, tapenade or shaved pastrami and béarnaise.

Place all ingredients in a food processor and mix until smooth and well combined. A little extra milk may be required if mixture is too thick. Ladle teaspoonfuls into a non-stick pan over medium heat or use an electric fry pan on medium heat. The first pikelet may require a tiny bit of light greasing of the fry pan but after that don't grease the pan between each batch and the pikelets will have a lovely golden brown surface. Cook both sides approximately 2 minutes each and cool on a wire rack.

CHEESE BISCUITS

Old-fashioned cheesy bickies for drinks parties.

150 grams butter
250 grams grated tasty cheese
1 1/2 cups flour
salt and freshly ground black pepper

Optional Extras
• Crushed corn chips or potato chips
• Sesame or poppy seeds
• Crushed cardamom
• Lemon pepper seasoning
• Cajun spice
• Sea salt flakes or coarsely ground rock salt
• Celery seeds

Mix all ingredients in food processor adding any optional extra flavourings. Shape into 2 x 20cm long logs. Wrap in plastic film and refrigerate for 20 minutes.

Preheat oven to 180°C. Cover a tray with a sheet of baking paper. Slice logs into 1cm thick rounds. Spread out on tray (sesame seeds, poppy seeds, rock salt etc. can be pressed into the surface of each biscuit). Bake 15 minutes until golden brown. Cool 2–3 minutes on tray then slide onto wire rack to cool completely. Store in airtight containers.

Top: Crispy cheese wrapped olive balls (see page 13)
Bottom: Old fashioned cheesy bickies for drinks, and bacon wheels (see page 12)

EASY SUSHI

Makes enough for 4 servings

A lot of culinary free rein has been taken here. I should stress this is very much Jo Seagar's interpretation of a Japanese art form.

1 1/2 cups short grain rice (Calrose or Japanese rice)
1 teaspoon salt
sushi-zu (special sushi rice vinegar, available at Asian supermarkets and delis)
6 nori sheets (Japanese dried seaweed)
4-6 slices of smoked salmon or fresh salmon fillet, finely sliced
1 firm avocado, peeled and sliced into strips
3 spring onions, green parts only, split lengthways
6–10 chives
wasabi paste (available in a tube from supermarkets or delis)
1 small package Japanese pickled ginger slices (about 20 slices)

Wash rice in cold running water then soak in fresh water for half an hour and then drain. Place rice in a medium-size saucepan (with a tight fitting lid) with 1 1/2 cups cold water and 1 teaspoon salt. Bring to the boil then turn to low and cook for 15 minutes. Cool with the lid on for a further 15 minutes. All the water will be absorbed and the rice clingy and sticky. Mix through 1/4 cup of sushi-zu and cool rice completely out on a flat tray.

To make sushi

Place a sheet of nori smooth side down on a bamboo mat or clean teatowel. Wet hands and place a handful of cooked sushi rice on the nori and smooth out to cover the nori except for a 3cm strip at the top edge. Spread a little wasabi, about 1/4 teaspoon paste, across the middle of the rice, then place smoked salmon (or thinly sliced fresh salmon) avocado, chives or spring onion greens and slices of pink pickled ginger. Roll up as tightly as possible using the bamboo mat. Wet the 3cm strip of nori with water and complete the roll. With wet fingers push in any loose rice at the ends. Wrap in plastic cling film and chill for at least an hour or up to 24 hours until you're ready to serve. Slice with a wet knife, wiping it between each cut. Slice into 6–8 pieces. Arrange on a serving platter or tray and serve with a dipping sauce of Japanese soy sauce mixed with a little wasabi paste.

Note: If you have trouble procuring the sushi-zu vinegar it can be made by mixing 1 tablespoon sugar and 1 teaspoon salt into 1/4 cup sherry and 1/4 cup rice vinegar, stirring until dissolved.

MINI COCKTAIL MUFFINS

Makes 3 dozen mini muffins

2 cups flour
4 teaspoons baking powder
1/2 teaspoon salt
1 egg
1/4 cup oil
1 1/4–1 1/2 cups milk
1 generous cup (a good handful) of grated cheese

Mix all ingredients in a large bowl until just blended together (don't overwork the mixture or the muffins will be too tough and chewy). Add enough milk to make a pourable (porridgy) consistency. Spoon into non-stick deep mini muffin tins. (I use Ecko bakeware, being very careful never to wash and scrub it. Just a wipe with a damp cloth and careful drying has the pans lasting for years.)

Bake at 200°C for about 15–18 minutes until golden brown. Tip out onto wire racks to cool.

Keep the fillings fairly moist to counter-balance the crispy dryness of the muffins. These provide good 'soaking up' food at a drinks party.

Suggested fillings
• Smoked salmon or trout with sour cream and caviar.
• Blue cheese and walnuts folded into sour cream or cream cheese.
• Chicken with ploughman's pickle and sour cream.
• Oysters with sour cream.

SMOKED SALMON PINWHEELS

Serves 4

A really quick and simple drinks nibble and a breeze to put together — but watch how fast they disappear.

100 gram pack (approx.) of smoked salmon slices
125 grams cream cheese, softened
1 teaspoon lemon pepper seasoning
1 tablespoon finely chopped parsley

Mash lemon pepper seasoning and parsley into soft cream cheese, then spread onto a slice of smoked salmon as if you were spreading butter on toast. Roll up tightly adding a second slice to the roll until it's as thick as a telegraph cucumber. With a clean knife, wiping the blade between each cut, slice into pinwheels and either serve as is or place on little squares of buttered ryebread.

Smoked salmon pinwheels and tiny pastry cases (see page 14–15) with smoked salmon and caviar

CAPER & SMOKED MUSSEL BABY QUICHE

Makes 36

3 sheets of frozen flaky puff pastry, thawed
1/2 cup grated cheese
1 small can smoked mussels, drained and chopped
(makes approx. 1/2 cup chopped mussels)
1 tablespoon capers, chopped finely
2 tablespoons chopped chives or parsley
1 teaspoon lemon pepper seasoning
3 eggs
1 cup cream

With a cookie cutter stamp out little circles 5–6cm diameter. Press into mini non-stick muffin tins. Sprinkle a few shreds of grated cheese into the base of each case. (This waterproofs the pastry bottoms of the baby quiches). Divide the chopped, smoked mussels, capers, chopped herbs and lemon pepper seasoning amongst the 36 cases. Whisk eggs and cream together and pour a little into each shell. Don't overfill. Bake in a preheated oven at 200°C until puffed and golden, about 20 minutes. Ease out of the muffin tins as soon as they're cool enough to handle and serve warm. These reheat beautifully. Serve these savouries just warm, not too hot as guests could easily burn their mouths on the hot filling.

Other filling ideas
• Crumbled blue cheese and roasted walnuts
• Leek and feta cheese
• Shrimp and lemon pepper
• Chargrilled pepper and black olives
• Button mushroom, brie and pinenuts

SPEEDY CROSTINI
& BRUSCHETTA

Crostini and bruschetta were designed as a means of using up day-old bread. I've experimented with all sorts of complicated ways of preparing them (cloves of garlic and drizzling extra virgin olive oil, etc.) but I've now come up with an easy-peasy way — spray olive oil.

spray olive oil (Bertolli make an excellent product)
day-old french bread sticks
garlic salt

Slice day-old french bread sticks into 1/2 cm thick slices for crostini or cut on the diagonal for bruschetta. Spray a baking tray liberally with olive oil spray, place a single layer of bread slices on this and again liberally spray the top with olive oil. Sprinkle with garlic salt and bake at 180°C until crisp and golden, about 10–15 minutes. Watch carefully as they burn quickly. Cool on a wire rack and store in an airtight container.

Topping ideas
I like to spread crostini with cream cheese first. This moistens them and provides a good 'palette' base for toppings. Be quite generous with the cream cheese — don't scrape it on meanly like marmite.

Top with:
• Chargrilled peppers and olive tapenade with parsley sprigs
• Smoked salmon and caviar
• Prawns and lemon pepper seasoning
• Avocado and pastrami
• Smoked chicken and mango chutney
• Smoked zucchini and fresh basil

SMALL COURSES

ZUCCHINI FRITTERS

500 grams (4 cups approx.) zucchini, coarsely grated
1 small onion, chopped finely
2 cloves garlic, crushed
75 grams parmesan cheese, grated
(substitute feta for variation)
3 eggs, beaten
breadcrumbs (extra for coating)
1/4 cup (approx.) chopped herbs
dill, chives, mint or parsley
freshly ground black pepper and salt, to taste
oil or clarified butter for frying

Mix all ingredients and form into small fritters 1cm thick with 6–7cm diameter, like a small crumpet. Dredge in extra breadcrumbs. Heat enough oil or clarified butter to generously cover the bottom of the frypan. Fry both sides until golden and drain on paper towels. Serve with a fruit chutney, tomato salsa or a dip.

A good dip can be made with green gherkin relish, piccalilli or mango chutney. Use 1 part pickle or relish with 2 parts sour cream or thick natural yoghurt.

POACHED EGGS ON PARMESAN ASPARAGUS NOODLES

2 spring onions, finely sliced
4 rashers of streaky bacon
6 fresh asparagus spears
250 grams broad pasta noodles
salt and freshly ground black pepper
1/2 cup cream
3 tablespoons freshly grated parmesan (plus extra to garnish)
4 poached eggs, to serve

Cut up bacon with scissors and trim and slice the asparagus. Cook pasta in boiling salted water until almost tender. Add asparagus to the water and return to boil. Cook 2–3 minutes until asparagus and pasta are tender and drain immediately. Meanwhile fry the bacon until crisp and golden. Add the spring onions and stir-fry for 1–2 minutes. Return the drained pasta and asparagus to the saucepan. Add spring onions and bacon mixture, cream, parmesan, salt and freshly ground black pepper. Toss lightly over low heat then serve topped with a poached egg and extra grated or shaved parmesan. (Shave parmesan from a block or wedge of cheese with a potato peeler).

A few little tips on perfect poached eggs.
• Always use fresh eggs – with an old egg the egg white and yolk separate as soon as it hits boiling water.
• Dip the whole egg (shell unbroken) in hot water for 30 seconds to start coagulating the egg white then break eggs into gently boiling water.
• Cover the pan for 3 minutes then remove eggs with a slotted spoon and serve immediately or keep warm in a dish with warm water just covering them.

CANNELLINI BEAN SOUP

Serves 4

People who love beans want a soup that doesn't contain anything else much but beans. This thick, tasty one fits the bill. It's actually thick enough to serve as a side dish to roast lamb, or thin it down for a more soupy consistency.

1/4 cup extra virgin olive oil
3 cloves garlic, crushed (1 heaped teaspoon)
2 cups of cooked drained and rinsed cannellini beans (canned beans are fine)
salt and freshly ground black pepper
1 1/2 cups (1 carton) beef stock
1/2 cup chopped fresh flat-leafed Italian parsley
toasted thick slices of crusty bread

Heat oil in a large saucepan, add garlic and cook 1–2 minutes. Add beans, salt and freshly ground black pepper and beef stock and simmer for 5 minutes. Purée half of the mixture in a blender or food processor and return to the saucepan and mix well with the remaining beans. Stir through the parsley and check the seasoning.

To serve: Place the slices of toasted bread in individual bowls and pour over the hot soup.

A grating of parmesan cheese is a nice garnish.

Cooking beans

To cook dried beans, first soak them overnight in water to cover. Drain, rinse and put the beans in a saucepan. Cover amply with water and simmer until tender, about 45 minutes to 1 hour. Salt the beans once they're fully cooked and store them refrigerated in their liquid.

Cannellini bean soup

HONEY LIME PRAWNS & SCALLOPS

Serves 4–6

750 grams green king prawns, shelled and deveined with tails left on
500 grams cleaned scallops
2 tablespoons of oil
3 tablespoons of clear liquid honey
juice and grated rind of 2 juicy limes, plus an extra lime sliced thinly for garnish
1 tablespoon of mint leaves, finely sliced

In a large frypan heat the oil. Add the prawns and scallops and stir-fry for 2–3 minutes until they start to change colour. Add honey, lime juice and rind and continue cooking for 2 more minutes until prawns and scallops are cooked through. Pile up onto individual serving plates and garnish with sliced mint and lime slices.

PUMPKIN SUCCOTASH SOUP

Serves 4–6

3–4 cups pumpkin purée (either peeled and deseeded pumpkin
boiled until soft, then puréed in a blender with milk,
or substitute pouch pack or canned pumpkin soup if in a super hurry)
1 can or 2 cups approx. of whole kernel sweetcorn
1 1/2 cups (1 can) approx. of soaked lima or white beans
salt and freshly ground black pepper
1 teaspoon of chilli sauce (or a few drops of a hot pepper sauce
like Kaitaia Fire or Tabasco), to taste
1/2 cup chopped herbs (parsley, chives etc.)
1–2 cups cream, or a mixture of milk and cream to thin the soup

Place all ingredients in a large saucepan and gently heat. Check the spiciness and seasoning and adjust to taste. The soup should be a thick stew-like consistency. Serve with crusty breads for a substantial first course or small meal.

CREAMY BLUE CHEESE & MUSHROOM SOUP

50 grams butter
250 grams mushrooms, chopped roughly or sliced (approx. 3 cups sliced)
1 small onion, roughly chopped
1 clove garlic, crushed
2 tablespoons flour
1 litre of chicken stock (or vegetable)
300 ml cream
200 ml milk
salt and freshly ground black pepper
100 grams of blue cheese
garnish — a few slices of mushrooms, crumbled blue cheese
and fresh herbs (chive flowers look great and have a good oniony taste)

Melt butter in a saucepan and add mushrooms, onion and garlic. Simmer, stirring for approximately 5 minutes, then add the flour and cook, stirring, another 2 minutes. Pour in the chicken stock and simmer for 10 minutes. Tip soup into a blender and purée with the milk, cream and blue cheese until smooth. Season to taste with salt and lots of freshly ground black pepper. Serve in individual bowls garnished with a few slices of mushroom, some crumbled blue cheese and a dusting of chopped herbs or chive petals, and lots of crusty bread.

For a complete, total cheat add the blue cheese and a few sliced mushrooms to a canned or 'made up to packet instructions, instant soup'. Add lots of freshly ground black pepper and garnish. A good slosh of sherry or brandy in the soup works well too.

CREOLE CHILLI PEANUT CHOWDER

Serves 4

A lovely creamy combination that really packs some great flavour.

50 grams butter
1 large onion, chopped finely
2 tablespoons flour
4 cups chicken stock
1 cup finely sliced celery
1 cup creamy peanut butter
1 cup cream
2 tablespoons sweet chilli sauce (or other type of chilli sauce, to taste)
juice and grated rind of 1 juicy lemon
salt and freshly ground black pepper
1/2 cup chopped roasted peanuts
1/2 cup chopped parsley

Melt the butter in a large saucepan over medium heat, add onion and cook until softened. Stir in flour and cook 2 minutes stirring constantly. Slowly add stock, stirring until smooth. Add celery, peanut butter, cream, sweet chilli sauce, lemon juice and grated rind. Reduce heat, cover and simmer gently for 10–15 minutes. Season with salt and freshly ground black pepper and pour into 4 soup plates. Spoon a swirl of sour cream into each serving and sprinkle with chopped roast peanuts and parsley.

Creole chilli peanut chowder

CHILLED FRESH ORANGE & PAWPAW SOUP

Serves 4

1 large ripe pawpaw, peeled, seeded and cut into chunks
juice and grated rind of 3 juicy oranges
(make up to 2 cups with cold water)
2 tablespoons finely sliced mint

In a blender working in batches purée the pawpaw, orange juice and grated rind. Chill and serve garnished with finely sliced mint in shallow bowls or soup cups. Parmesan wafers or cheesy biscuits are a nice accompaniment.

CRUMBED BRIE

Cut the brie cheeses into 6 or 8 wedges each. Place the flour in a plastic bag and toss the brie wedges in the flour. Beat the eggs until smooth and frothy. Dip the floured brie wedges into the egg then into the breadcrumbs until well coated. Repeat the egg and breadcrumbing so they have 2 coats of crumbs. Place on a plate in the fridge and chill for at least 1 hour.

To make the dressing: Whisk all ingredients in a blender or food processor until well combined.

To serve: Toss the salad leaves in a bowl with half the dressing. Place a handful of dressed salad leaves on 4 individual plates. Deep-fry the brie wedges 3–4 minutes until golden brown and divide amongst the salad plates, 3–4 pieces each. Garnish with fruit and the pecans and pour a little extra dressing over the top. Serve immediately.

CRUMBED BRIE ON SALAD WITH HONEY DIJON DRESSING & PECANS

Serves 4

2 x 125 gram small wheels of brie cheese
1/2 cup flour
3 eggs
1 cup breadcrumbs
oil for deep frying
4 handfuls of mixed salad leaves or mesclun mix
1/2 cup pecan nuts, toasted

Dressing

1 cup soya oil
2 tablespoons dijon style smooth mustard
2 tablespoons white wine vinegar
1 tablespoon liquid honey
salt and freshly ground black pepper to taste
2–3 tablespoons chopped parsley

Optional Extras

• Sliced fresh peach or nectarine
• Sliced pawpaw or melon
• Sliced strawberries

HAYMAKER PICNIC PIES

Makes 12

These are quicker to prepare and cook than traditional bacon and egg pies for picnics but certainly run along the same principle. They're easy to handle and look like you've gone to a lot of extra trouble by making individual servings whereas they're actually easier to make. A wonderful lunchtime dish and a great vehicle for any leftovers you find in the fridge.

3 sheets frozen flaky pastry, thawed
1 cup approx. grated cheese
1 cup ham or chopped crispy cooked bacon
4-5 gherkins or pickled onions, finely chopped
2 tablespoons finely chopped parsley
2 cups cream
6 eggs
extra chopped parsley to garnish

Preheat oven to 200°C. With a large cookie cutter cut circles of pastry approximately 12 cm diameter and press into deep non-stick muffin tins. Don't worry if pastry overlaps a little. Sprinkle a few shreds of grated cheese into the base of each case (this waterproofs the bases), then divide ham or bacon and gherkins or pickled onions between the cases. Sprinkle over salt and freshly ground black pepper and finely chopped parsley. Beat cream and eggs together and pour a little into each case, being careful not to spill over the sides or overfill. Top each pie with a few shreds of grated cheese. Bake until golden and puffed up with the egg filling set, about 25 minutes. Ease out of the muffin tins as soon as they are cool enough to handle. Best served warm.

Variations
• Pine nut and basil
• Finely shredded spinach and feta cheese
• Red onion and chopped fresh herbs
• Blue cheese and walnuts
• Smoked fish and a little horseradish in the cream
• Mussels or any shellfish with a little chopped parsley
• Diced red, green and yellow pepper and chilli flakes
• Camembert cheese and strawberries with ground black peppercorns
• Pickled walnuts and tasty cheddar

Haymaker picnic pies

CARAWAY SWEET ONION TARTS

Serves 4

100 grams butter
1 large onion, finely chopped (Pacific Sweet or Sweet Texas type)
1 teaspoon sugar
2 eggs
150 grams (approx. 1 cup) sour cream
salt and freshly ground black pepper
2 sheets of frozen flaky puff pastry, thawed
2 teaspoons caraway seeds

Preheat oven to 200°C. Melt butter in a heavy pan over medium heat. Add onion and sugar and sauté for approximately 10 minutes until the onion is golden and translucent. Beat eggs and sour cream together, season with salt and lots of freshly ground black pepper. Cut pastry sheets in half on a large baking tray. Fold pastry edges up to form a little 1/2 cm ridge. Spoon onions into the pastry spreading evenly. Pour sour cream mix over and sprinkle with caraway seeds. Bake until puffed and golden and the cream mixture is set, about 30–35 minutes. Serve warm.

Note: If you can't get Pacific Sweet or Sweet Texas onions, use a regular onion but increase the sugar from 1 to 2 teaspoons.

ANCHOVY STUFFED MUSHROOMS

Serves 4

12 medium to large flat open mushrooms
(the brown gourmet mushrooms are particularly meaty and tasty for this dish)
50 grams butter
1 tablespoon olive oil
6 spring onions, white parts only, finely sliced
1 clove garlic, crushed
2 rashers rindless bacon, chopped
2 anchovy fillets, chopped
3 tablespoons chopped parsley
1 cup fresh white breadcrumbs
1/2 cup white wine
juice and grated rind of 1 lemon

Preheat oven 180°C. In a large frypan heat butter and oil. Stir-fry spring onions, garlic, bacon, anchovies, parsley, breadcrumbs and 4 of the mushrooms finely chopped for 3–4 minutes until crumbs are golden. Add wine, lemon juice and grated rind, stirring to moisten crumbs. Spoon mixture into the remaining 8 mushroom caps and place these on a baking tray.

Bake 12–15 minutes until the mushroom caps are tender. Garnish with extra parsley sprigs.

Oysters

Oysters should smell fresh and of the sea. They shouldn't be slimy but glossy, plump and clear. Oysters on the half shell freeze really well with little loss of texture, plumpness and flavour. Quickly thaw them by placing in salted fresh water then serve either natural with a squeeze of lemon and freshly ground black pepper or in one of these ways.

OYSTERS SERVED HOT WITH LEMON PEPPER CRUMBS

1 cup fresh breadcrumbs
1 teaspoon lemon pepper seasoning
1/2 teaspoon paprika
50 grams butter, melted

Toss all ingredients together and spread on a baking tray. Bake at 180°C for about 15 minutes until crisp and golden. Squeeze a juicy lemon or lime over oysters on the half shell and sprinkle with breadcrumbs. Bake for 5 minutes to heat through.

ORIENTAL DRESSING FOR OYSTERS

1/2 cup rice vinegar
1 teaspoon minced fresh ginger
1 spring onion (the green part only), finely sliced
1 teaspoon grated lemon rind
2 teaspoons soy sauce

Whisk together with a fork and serve over oysters on the half shell.

Top: Oysters with lemon pepper crumbs. Right: Mustard dill cream (see page 44). Left: Oriental dressing

MUSTARD DILL CREAM

1 tablespoon smooth dijon style mustard
150 grams (1 small cup approx.) sour cream
1 tablespoon of chopped fresh dill
dill sprigs to garnish

Mix all together and place a teaspoon on each oyster on half shell and garnish with a dill sprig.

NOODLE FRITTERS WITH SMOKED SALMON & CAVIAR

Serves 4

2 x 85 gram packets 2 minute noodles (any flavour)
3 eggs, beaten
1 cup grated cheese
salt and pepper
oil for shallow frying
To serve: *sliced smoked salmon, caviar or lumpfish roe, sour cream, parsley sprigs for garnish*

Cook noodles as per packet instructions. Drain well, place in a large mixing bowl and add eggs, grated cheese and salt and pepper. Mix well. Heat oil in a large heavy-based frypan over medium heat. Using kitchen tongs, pick up approximately 1/2 cup of noodle mixture and place in the pan to form small fritters. Cook for about 3 minutes each side until golden crispy brown. Drain on paper towels and keep warm while you cook remaining fritters.

Serve with dollops of sour cream, caviar and sliced smoked salmon. Garnish with sprigs of fresh herbs.

THAI PRAWN
& LEMONGRASS SOUP

Serves 4

1 tablespoon oil
1 large onion, finely chopped
2 cloves garlic, crushed
1 teaspoon crushed ginger
2 tablespoons Thai curry paste
1 x 400 ml can of coconut cream
1 1/2 cups (approx. 1 x 500 gram carton) fish or chicken stock
2 teaspoons crushed lemongrass stems
3 cups approx. green or uncooked prawns, peeled and deveined
salt and freshly ground black pepper to taste
1/2 cup fresh coriander, chopped
2 spring onions, finely sliced

Heat oil in a large saucepan, add onion and cook until softened 2–3 minutes. Add garlic, ginger and curry paste and cook for a further minute. While stirring add coconut cream, fish stock and lemongrass, simmer for 10–15 minutes covered. Add prawns, coriander and spring onions, season with salt and freshly ground black pepper. Serve immediately.

GREEK STYLE CHICKEN & LEMON SOUP
(Avgolemono Soup)

Serves 4

Chicken soup is a cure for world-weariness and here's an even better chicken soup than Mother used to make (unless of course your mother is Greek, in which case she probably makes this one).

6 cups well-flavoured chicken stock
(use either homemade, canned, carton or make up from chicken stock powder)
1 chicken breast, with skin and bones removed
1 tablespoon chopped parsley
1/2 cup short grain rice (Calrose brand rice works well)
3 eggs
grated rind and juice of 3–4 juicy medium sized lemons

Bring the stock, rice and chicken breast gently to the boil. Turn down the heat and simmer for 10 minutes. Check that the rice is cooked and with kitchen tongs or a slotted spoon, remove the cooked chicken breast. Shred the chicken meat and return to the stock. Add a little water to return the volume to approximately the original 6 cups. In a medium-sized bowl, beat eggs, lemon juice and the grated rind. Slowly add a cup of the hot stock to the egg mixture as you contin-uously whisk. Remove the saucepan of stock from the heat and stir the egg mixture into the saucepan. Add the parsley and serve immediately.

DO NOT return to the heat or try to heat up the soup, as the egg curdles and sets solid like scrambled egg. To make this soup more of a substantial meal, add more chicken meat and green vegetables and serve with crusty bread.

FRESH BASIL & TOMATO SOUP

(A cunning title as the basil is fresh, the tomato is canned)

This soup should be a thick peasant-style dish. Garnish with shaved parmesan (use a potato peeler) and lots of crusty bread. All sorts of bits and pieces can be added to this soup — leftover vegetables, peas, beans, chopped up potatoes, rice, bits of ham or bacon, chicken pieces. A great dish for 'going through the fridge'.

2 tablespoons olive oil
1 large onion, roughly chopped
2 cloves garlic, crushed (1 teaspoon)
2 x 400 gram cans of peeled tomatoes in juice
2 cups of tomato juice or chicken stock
1/2 cup small dried pasta, such as macaroni
1/2 cup (approx.) telegraph cucumber, diced
1/2 cup celery, finely sliced
salt to taste, and at least 1 teaspoon freshly ground black pepper
1 teaspoon worcestershire sauce
3 tablespoons chopped fresh basil
3 tablespoons chopped fresh parsley
shaved parmesan and crusty bread, to serve

Heat olive oil in a large pan, add onions and cook 2–3 minutes. Add garlic, the canned tomatoes and their juice, the chicken stock or tomato juice, and the pasta. Simmer gently until the pasta is soft. Add the cucumber and celery, salt and freshly ground black pepper and worcestershire, then stir in the herbs. Serve immediately.

SMOKED SEAFOOD CHOWDER

Serves 4–6

1 x 310 gram can of smoked fish fillets, or 2 cups of flaked smoked fish
2 cups (approx.) mixed seafood
(prawns, smoked mussels, oysters, white fish fillets etc.)
100 grams butter
1 leek, finely sliced
1 tablespoon flour
1 cup fish stock (use the liquid from the canned smoked fish fillets)
1 cup milk
1 potato, peeled and diced into small pea-size pieces
1 cup sweetcorn (fresh off the cob, frozen, canned or cream style)
1/2 cup cream
salt and freshly ground black pepper

Heat the butter in a large saucepan and add the sliced leek. Stir-fry 3–4 minutes then add the flour and stir well. Simmer over gentle heat while constantly stirring and add the fish stock and milk. Add the corn, diced potato, smoked fish and other seafood. Gently simmer until the potato is softened and the soup is smooth and thick. Finally add cream and season to taste with freshly ground black pepper and a little salt (note that smoked fish tends to be quite salty).

MAINS

CHARGRILLED PEPPER & SPINACH STUFFED CHICKEN BREASTS ON COUSCOUS WITH SWEET CHILLI YOGHURT SAUCE

Serves 4

4 single, boneless chicken breasts, with skin on
4 thick strips of chargrilled pepper (approx. 1 pepper – Kato Pacific peppers
packed in oil are very handy for this)
4-6 long rashers rindless bacon
4 spinach leaves
garlic salt to sprinkle over

Place a strip of chargrilled pepper and a spinach leaf under each chicken breast. Wrap each chicken breast skin side up with a bacon rasher in a figure of eight pattern. Sprinkle with garlic salt. Bake at 180°C for approximately 25–30 minutes, until the bacon is crisp and the chicken skin crisp and golden. Serve on a bed of couscous with sweet chilli yoghurt sauce.

Note: The skin left on the chicken prevents it drying out while cooking.

Stuffed chicken breasts, couscous and sweet chilli yogurt sauce

SWEET CHILLI YOGHURT SAUCE

A simply put together sauce with tons of uses which keeps covered in fridge 2–3 days.

500 ml natural, sweetened yoghurt
3 cloves garlic, crushed (1 teaspoon)
1/2 cup chopped parsley
1 teaspoon sweet chilli sauce

Mix all together, cover and chill.

COUSCOUS

Serves 4

2 cups couscous grain
2 cups water or chicken stock
1 teaspoon salt
1 tablespoon olive oil
a generous knob of butter
1/2 cup chopped parsley
1 tablespoon sweet chilli sauce

Boil water, add salt, oil, couscous and butter. Turn off heat, stir for a few seconds and allow grain to absorb the liquid. Fluff up with a fork before serving and mix in parsley and sweet chilli sauce. Can be reheated by microwaving or adding a little boiling water and mixing through.

Other couscous flavouring ideas
• Rice seasoning mixes (McCormack Thai lemongrass chilli and coconut is extremely good)
• Fresh chopped herbs
• Lemon pepper with lemon juice
• Orange juice and orange zest
• Chopped olives, dried tomatoes and fresh basil

POTATO & PLOUGHMAN'S PICKLE SELF CRUSTING PIE

Serves 6-8

This is a really tasty pie where you throw it all in together and don't have to fiddle around with pastry. It makes a great luncheon or supper dish that reheats beautifully so it can be prepared ahead of time when entertaining a crowd.

2 large onions
2–3 cloves garlic, crushed
50 grams butter
4 eggs
1 cup milk
1/2 cup self-raising flour
3 medium cooked potatoes, cut up into 1 cm cubes
2 cups small button mushrooms, sliced in half
3 tablespoons piccalilli (or any kind of chutney or relish)
1 1/2 cups grated cheese
1 tablespoon chopped parsley
2–3 small tomatoes
salt and pepper, to taste

Melt the butter in a small saucepan or in the microwave and cook the onion and garlic until soft. Whisk in the eggs and milk then stir in the flour, piccalilli and grated cheese. Mix in the potato cubes, mushrooms, chopped parsley and season to taste with salt and pepper. Pour into an oblong lasagne-type dish that has been well greased. Garnish with tomato slices. I use and thoroughly recommend the new non-stick glass dishes. Metal or china may be used but don't use a loose-bottomed dish. Bake at 220°C for 25–30 minutes until lightly browned and set in the middle. Turn out onto a board to serve.

LAMB TAGINE

Serves 6–8

A tagine is actually the dish in which slowly-simmered North African stews are cooked. However over time the word tagine has come to mean this style of dish.

*1 kilo lean lamb, preferably cut from the shoulder
and cubed into 2–3 cm pieces
3 tablespoons oil
1 large onion, roughly chopped
6 cloves (2 teaspoons) of garlic, crushed
1 teaspoon cinnamon
1 tablespoon fresh tarragon chopped, or 1 teaspoon dried
2 teaspoons ground cumin
1 1/2 cups water or chicken stock
1 cup freshly squeezed orange juice
1 teaspoon grated orange rind
15 pitted prunes (Sunsweet orange-flavoured prunes
are particularly good with the citrus flavours of this dish)
2 tablespoons clear liquid honey
salt and freshly ground black pepper, to taste
1/4 cup almonds, blanched
1/4 cup sesame seeds
1/4 cup raisins*

Heat oil in a large frypan. Add lamb, onion and garlic, stir over medium heat for 3-4 minutes then add the spices and herbs, water, orange juice and grated rind. Stir to mix well and pour into a large covered casserole. Bake for 1 1/2 hours at 160°C. Stir every now and then and add more water if the mixture is getting too dry. Season to taste with salt and freshly ground black pepper, add the liquid honey and prunes. Cook 10 more minutes to soften prunes. In a small frypan, with just a tiny splash of oil, fry the almonds and sesame seeds until golden brown. Add the raisins, swirl the pan around to warm them then sprinkle them over the meat mixture. Serve with rice or couscous.

Lamb tagine

PUMPKIN HAZELNUT BUTTER RISOTTO

Serves 4

Hazelnut Butter
1/2 cup hazelnuts, toasted and shelled
125 grams butter, softened
1/2 cup chopped parsley
salt and freshly ground black pepper

Pumpkin Risotto
100 grams butter
2 medium onions, chopped
500 grams (approx. 4 cups) pumpkin peeled, deseeded and cut into1cm cubes
3 cloves garlic, crushed
1 1/2 cups risotto (Arborio) rice
600 ml hot chicken stock
juice and grated rind of 1 orange
1 cup approx. shaved (use a potato peeler) fresh parmesan cheese

Finely chop the hazelnuts and using a fork mash together with the butter. Mix in the chopped parsley and salt and freshly ground black pepper to taste. Roll into a sausage shape in a piece of tinfoil or plastic wrap and chill.

Heat butter in a large sauté or deep frypan. Cook the onion until soft and transparent. Add the pumpkin and sauté over gentle heat for 6–8 minutes until just beginning to soften. Add the crushed garlic, rice, orange juice and grated rind. Stir to mix well. Turn heat up slightly to medium and add the hot chicken stock, a little at a time, stirring constantly, allowing the liquid to be absorbed after each addition. This will take 20–25 minutes. The rice should be tender but firm to the bite and should be creamily bound together.

Cut the hazelnut butter into thin slices and serve the risotto with slices of hazelnut butter melting over the top. Garnish the dish with shaved parmesan and extra finely shredded orange peel.

GRILLED LEMON CORIANDER CHICKEN

Serves 4

2 lemons
1/2 cup chopped fresh coriander, plus a few leaves to garnish
2 cloves of garlic crushed
2 tablespoons white wine
2 tablespoons olive oil
1 tablespoon liquid clear honey
4 chicken breasts, boned out but with the skin on
salt and freshly ground black pepper
5 thin spring onions, sliced diagonally
lemon slices to garnish

Grate the rind and squeeze the juice of the lemons. Mix this with the coriander, crushed garlic, wine, oil and honey. Add a generous amount of freshly ground black pepper and salt to taste. Coat the boned chicken breasts with this mixture. Line a grill pan with tinfoil (makes for an easy clean up) and grill chicken for 10 minutes approximately each side until cooked through and golden crisp. Baste with the marinade. To serve, spoon any remaining pan juices over the chicken and sprinkle with the sliced spring onions and reserved coriander leaves.

Serve with lemon couscous.

CUMIN SPICED SEARED LAMB

Serves 4

500–600 grams cubed lean lamb
(from lamb fillets or slices of lamb loin cut into approx. 1 cm cubes)
1 small onion, grated or finely chopped in a food processor
2 cloves of garlic, crushed (1 teaspoon)
1 teaspoon ground cumin
1 teaspoon ground paprika
1/2 teaspoon chilli powder
1/2 cup finely chopped fresh coriander
1/4 cup olive oil
grated rind and juice of 1 medium juicy lemon

Place lamb in a dish or bowl. Mix all the ingredients and stir through the lamb. Cover and refrigerate, marinating lamb for at least 2 hours, longer for a stronger flavour. Grill or sear the meat on a BBQ hotplate or in a hot heavy metal pan. The meat should be crisp and browned on the outside and pink inside — 3–4 minutes should do it.

Serve in pita bread or tortillas, or over couscous or rice with sweet chilli yoghurt sauce (see page 52).

Cumin spiced seared lamb in pita bread

FISH FILLETS WITH FRESH BREADCRUMBS & LEMON ZEST CRUST

Serves 4

4 fish fillets, skinned and boned
(tarakihi, snapper, wild trout or salmon)
2 lemons
1/4 cup chopped fresh herbs
(parsley, dill, tarragon, chives)
1/2 cup fresh breadcrumbs
(whizz 2 slices of thick toast bread in the food processor)
50 grams butter
salt and freshly ground black pepper

Remove as many bones from the fish fillets as possible and place fillets in a greased baking dish. Finely grate the lemon rind and toss this with salt and freshly ground black pepper, the breadcrumbs and herbs. Press this crumb mixture into the top side of the fish fillets. Melt the butter, add the squeezed lemon juice and pour over the crumbed fish and bake in a preheated oven at 220°C for 12–15 minutes or place under the grill for 6–8 minutes.

FISH FILLETS WITH A SPICY YOGHURT CRUST

Serves 4

4 fish fillets
1 clove garlic, crushed (1/2 teaspoon)
1 teaspoon ginger, freshly grated
1/2 teaspoon ground cumin
1/2 teaspoon ground coriander
1 teaspoon sweet chilli sauce
1 cup of plain natural yoghurt

Mix garlic, ginger, cumin, coriander, chilli sauce and yoghurt. Place fish fillets in the yoghurt mix, cover and refrigerate for 2-3 hours. Cover a grill pan with tin foil (makes for an easier clean up) and place fish in the pan and under a hot grill for 6-8 minutes until the fish is cooked through. Season with freshly ground black pepper and garnish with either flat leaf parsley or fresh coriander sprigs and lemon or lime wedges.

Serve with couscous or rice and a salad.

SALMON PRAWN SALAD IN TORTILLA BASKETS

Serves 4

Your own homemade tortilla baskets create a dramatic presentation for a salad, entrée or main course. They can also be used for serving chilli or beans when you want to take it to a culinary high. They look great but are easy to do.

250 grams cooked boneless salmon fillet or hot smoked salmon
1 cup of cooked prawns
4 handfuls of mesclun mix or mixed baby salad leaves
1 cup fresh strawberries, halved
1 avocado, peeled and sectioned
2 oranges, peeled and sectioned
1/2 cup toasted macadamia nuts or almonds

Dressing
juice and grated rind of 1 juicy lemon
1/2 cup olive oil
salt and freshly ground black pepper
1 teaspoon brown sugar
1 tablespoon white wine vinegar

Mix all together in a large bowl. Lightly toss salad ingredients with dressing then divide into the tortilla baskets.

To make tortilla baskets

Lightly brush (or spray) both sides of 4 flour tortillas and press into muffin tins or into small ovenproof bowls. Place a small ball of tinfoil crumpled into the base of each tortilla and bake at 180°C for 15–20 minutes approximately until light golden brown. Remove the foil and cool tortillas in the mould. When cool enough to handle remove from the mould and fill with the salmon prawn salad (or other salad of your choice) and dress at the last moment. Serve immediately or they will go soft and limp. If not used immediately the baskets can be stored in an airtight container for up to 5 days.

Tortilla baskets with salmon and prawn salad

ROAST LAMB WITH ROSEMARY & ANCHOVY

An old Scottish recipe that sounds a bit unusual, mixing fish and lamb, but is really worth trying. The anchovies make a gorgeous crust on the lamb and a delicious gravy is made with the pan drippings.

1 leg of lamb
1 small can or jar of anchovies (approximately 12 anchovies)
6 cloves garlic, each clove sliced into 2 or 3 pieces
2 tablespoons fresh rosemary leaves

In a small bowl, mash together with a fork the anchovies and rosemary leaves, adding a little of the anchovy oil if necessary, to form a thick paste. Cut small slits in the lamb and insert the pieces of garlic. Score the lamb with a sharp knife and spread the paste thickly over.

MUSTARD PORK STROGANOFF

Serves 4

2 tablespoons oil
2 medium onions, sliced
2–3 pork fillets, depending on size (about 700 grams),
cut into strips like french fries
250 grams (approx. 3 cups) button mushrooms, sliced
3 tablespoons grainy mustard
250 grams sour cream
1/2 cup white wine
salt and freshly ground black pepper

Heat the oil in a large frypan, add onions and stir-fry until starting to caramelise golden brown. Remove from pan and add the pork, stir-frying over high heat until brown. Add onions back to the pan with the mushrooms. Season with salt and lots of freshly ground black pepper, add wine and stir for 3 minutes. Lower heat and stir in the mustard and sour cream. Let the sauce bubble and reduce down. Serve immediately over rice or buttered noodles.

TANDOORI STYLE
BUTTER CHICKEN & MUSHROOMS

Serves 4

3 double chicken breasts, skin and bones removed
3 tablespoons approx. tandoori paste (tandoori paste in jars available at
supermarkets and delis – Pataks and Sharwoods are good brands or
you can use dry tandoori seasoning powder)
2 tablespoons oil
1 tablespoon white wine vinegar
100 grams butter
2 onions, chopped roughly
250 grams (approx. 3 cups sliced) button mushrooms
1/2 cup chopped parsley
1/2 cup chopped fresh coriander
500 grams (2 cups) sour cream or thick natural yoghurt
(extra chopped parsley and coriander to garnish)

Cut up chicken into bite-size pieces and place in a casserole dish. Mix tandoori paste with oil and white wine vinegar and stir into chicken, coating well. Leave covered in fridge for at least 3–4 hours (preferably overnight).

Heat oven to 200°C. Heat butter in small pan or microwave, cook onion to soften. Add to chicken and mix in mushrooms, parsley, coriander and half of the sour cream or yoghurt. Bake about 20 minutes until chicken has cooked through. Stir in remaining sour cream or yoghurt, mix well to blend in and sprinkle with extra herbs to garnish. Serve with couscous, rice or buttered noodles.

Tandoori style butter chicken and mushrooms

CHICKEN GINGER STIR-FRY WITH TOMATO & MINT

Serves 4

3 tablespoons soy sauce
2 tablespoons hoisin sauce
4 boneless skinless chicken breasts, cut into strips (like french fries)
2 tablespoons sesame oil
1 tablespoon chopped fresh ginger
2 small zucchini, thinly sliced
5 spring onions
1 small can water chestnuts, drained and sliced (approx. 1/2–3/4 cup)
a handful of small green beans, topped and tailed
(frozen beans are fine)
3 medium tomatoes, seeds removed, chopped into small dice
1 tablespoon chopped mint
salt and pepper

Mix soy and hoisin sauces in small bowl. Season chicken with salt and pepper. Heat sesame oil in large heavy frypan over high heat, add ginger and stir for 15 seconds, add chicken slices and stir-fry 2 minutes. Add zucchini, spring onions, water chestnuts and beans and stir-fry until chicken and vegetables are tender, about 3 minutes. Add the soy and hoisin sauces and toss to mix well. Transfer to a serving dish and sprinkle with the tomato dice and chopped mint. Serve with Asian noodles or rice.

CHICKEN BREASTS WITH PORT, DRIED CURRANTS & CREAM

Serves 4

4 chicken breasts
(bone in or boneless as desired, legs would be fine as well)
2 cloves garlic, crushed (1 teaspoon)
1/2 cup chopped parsley
grated rind and juice of 2 lemons
2 tablespoons olive oil
1/2 teaspoon salt and a generous grind of black pepper
1 tablespoon smooth dijon style mustard
1 1/2 cups port
1/2 cup balsamic vinegar
1/2 cup dried currants
1 cup cream
50 grams butter
250 grams (3 cups approx.) button mushrooms, sliced

In a food processor mix garlic, parsley, lemon juice and grated rind, oil, mustard, salt and freshly ground black pepper to a coarse paste. Rub paste over the chicken breasts, place in a plastic bag and marinate for at least 6 hours overnight. Bake chicken at 200°C until crisp and cooked through, about 30 minutes. Meanwhile in a small saucepan bring port and vinegar to the boil. Add currants and remove from heat. Rest about 15 minutes until they have plumped up and softened. Add cream and cook over medium heat until sauce has reduced by half. Heat butter in a large frypan, add mushrooms and sauté for 3 minutes. Place chicken on a serving plate, spoon sauce over and garnish with the sautéed mushrooms.

FARMER'S COUNTRY STYLE FRITTATA

Serves 4–6

Any combination of vegetables may be used — zucchini and pumpkin are particularly good. A frittata is a good way of dealing with the loaves-and-fishes syndrome when you appear to have an empty fridge but company has arrived. I've even plumped mine out with cooked rice or leftover pasta.

1 tablespoon oil
4 rashers of rindless bacon, chopped into small pieces
1 large onion, finely chopped
2 cloves garlic, crushed (1/2 teaspoon)
3 medium potatoes, scrubbed and diced into 1 cm pieces
1 cup (approx.) button mushrooms, sliced
1 small red pepper, deseeded and finely chopped
2–3 tablespoons chopped parsley
salt and freshly ground black pepper
2 cups grated cheese (reserve 1/2 cup for sprinkling over)
6 large eggs
1/4 cup cream (or milk)

Heat the oil in a medium frypan, preferably non-stick. Fry the bacon until brown and crisp. Add the onion, garlic and potato cubes and stir-fry until the potato is soft, about 5–6 minutes. Add the mushrooms, pepper and parsley. Season with salt and freshly ground black pepper to taste and stir through the grated cheese. In a separate bowl beat the eggs and cream together and pour over the mixture. Turn heat down to low and cook for about 4 minutes until the bottom is golden crisp and the centre setting. The top should still be rather wet and uncooked. Remove pan from the heat, sprinkle the reserved grated cheese over the top and place under a grill to brown for 3–4 minutes. Cut into wedges and serve immediately.

Farmer's country style frittata

CHICKEN CAESAR SALAD

Serves 4

4 single chicken breasts, bones removed but with skin still on
1 teaspoon garlic salt seasoning
3 tablespoons oil
1 large romaine or other crisp lettuce
2 cups cubed chunky toast bread (french bread is best)
1/2 cup approx. shaved parmesan cheese
4 poached eggs

Dressing
2 tablespoons olive oil
10 anchovies
3 cloves garlic, crushed (1 teaspoon)
juice and grated rind of a juicy lemon
1 cup cream
1/4 cup grated parmesan cheese

Dressing
In a small pan heat oil, add anchovies and garlic and cook 2–3 minutes. Add the lemon juice and grated rind, cream and parmesan. Turn off heat and when cool whizz in a blender. Store in a sealed container in fridge 2–3 days.

Sprinkle chicken breasts with garlic salt seasoning. Heat oil in a large pan and add the chicken breasts, pan-fry for 4–5 minutes each side over medium heat until cooked through. Remove chicken and in the same pan toss the breadcrumbs, pan-fry until golden. Slice chicken breasts.

Toss salad leaves with the dressing. Mix in sliced chicken, hot croûtons and shaved parmesan. Season with lots of freshly ground black pepper and place in 4 individual serving bowls. Top each individual serving with a lightly poached egg.

KASHMIR SPICED LAMB PANCAKE PARCELS

Serves 4

Basic Pancake Mixture
3 eggs
1 1/2 cups milk
1 cup flour
1/4 cup oil
salt and pepper

Mix all of the ingredients in a blender or food processor and ladle a spoonful of mixture into a hot non-stick crêpe pan. Swirl around to evenly coat the bottom of the pan and carefully turn over as the crêpe surface appears cooked and dry. The second side takes only a few seconds to finish. Stack up on a wire rack and place baking paper between each pancake to prevent sticking together. Reheat the pan and repeat process with remaining mixture.

Spiced Lamb Filling
400 grams minced lamb
1 packet leek and potato soup mix powder
1 tablespoon (or to taste) mild curry powder (eg Maggi)
1/2 cup coarsely shredded coconut
1/2 cup (a small handful) of sultanas
1/2 cup chopped parsley
salt and freshly ground black pepper
1 cup sweetened natural yoghurt (if you only have unsweetened yoghurt
add a teaspoon of liquid honey)

Sprinkle minced lamb with a packet of leek and potato soup mix, a tablespoon of mild curry powder and salt and pepper. Microwave or cook, stirring often until the mince has lost its pinkness. No extra liquid is required and the meat juices are absorbed by the soup powder. Add coconut and sultanas and stir through a cup of sweetened natural yoghurt. Place the mixture on the paler side of the pancake and fold into little parcels. Serve with extra natural sweetened yoghurt on the side.

General Pasta Tips

When serving your guests pasta remember the more complicated the shape of the pasta the more impressed your guests will be. You get more points serving tortellini or farfalle, the little butterfly or bowtie shapes, than plain macaroni or spaghetti. I nearly always serve small pasta shapes rather than long fettuccine and spaghetti, just because it's so much easier to deal to with a fork and saves all that drycleaning of white silk shirts, which is invariably what I'm wearing when I lose a strand of 'spag' en route to my mouth.

Don't be put off serving pasta and noodles when entertaining, thinking that it involves a lot of last-minute cooking. Do what the cafés and restaurants do and cook pasta ahead of time until it's just tender (al dente), drain, lightly rinse and mix through a little oil tossing carefully to coat the pasta and prevent sticking. To reheat either microwave 2–3 minutes, covered, or pour over boiling water for a minute.

SPINACH TORTELLINI WITH BACON MUSHROOMS & SWEET CHILLI

Serves 4

250 gram (packet) of fresh ricotta-stuffed spinach tortellini (Pasta Fresca brand is excellent)
4–6 bacon rashers, crisply cooked and chopped up
1 cup button mushrooms, sliced
1/4 –1/2 cup cream
2 teaspoons sweet chilli sauce
salt and freshly ground black pepper
2 tablespoons chopped parsley

Boil pasta in lots of salted water until tender. Drain and into the hot saucepan toss the chopped cooked bacon, mushrooms, sweet chilli sauce and cream. Cook for 2 minutes, season to taste with salt and freshly ground black pepper. Return the pasta and add parsley. Mix well and serve immediately. If desired shave off a few shreds of fresh parmesan to garnish.

Spinach tortellini with bacon mushrooms and sweet chilli sauce, with food-processor focaccia bread

PASTA WITH GORGONZOLA & WALNUT SAUCE

Serves 4

50 grams butter
5 spring onions, finely sliced
1 tablespoon fresh chopped thyme (or 1 teaspoon dried thyme)
1/2 cup coarsely chopped parsley
300 ml cream
250 grams gorgonzola blue cheese, crumbled (or substitute a firm blue cheese
like blue vein which is much cheaper and works just as well)
freshly ground black pepper
400 grams dried pasta, about 3 cups depending on pasta size,
fusilli, penne or farfale
1 cup walnut pieces, toasted
1/2 cup shaved parmesan cheese

Melt butter in heavy frypan over medium heat, add spring onions and sauté for 5 minutes. Add fresh thyme, parsley and pour in the cream, stir until it bubbles and starts to boil. Reduce heat and stir in crumbled blue cheese (reserve a little for the garnish) until melted. Turn off heat. Boil pasta in a large saucepan of salted water, drain. Place pasta back in the hot saucepan and toss the sauce through it with the walnuts. Spoon into 4 individual serving bowls, garnish with shaved parmesan and reserved crumbled blue cheese.

BLACK TIE PASTA

Serves 4

3–4 cups of bowtie or farfale dried pasta
100 grams butter
5 spring onions, finely sliced
1 clove garlic, crushed
5–6 smoked salmon slices, cut into fine strips (or approx. 1 cup of hot smoked salmon
or smoked trout fillets, flaked)
1/4 cup vodka
1 1/2 cups cream (300 ml approx.)
freshly ground black pepper, to taste
1 cup baby frozen peas
a small jar of black lump fish roe (caviar) (about 2 tablespoons)
5–6 chives, chopped, to garnish

Cook pasta in a large saucepan of salted boiling water until tender and drain. Into the hot pasta saucepan add the butter, spring onions and garlic and stir-fry for 2 minutes. Add the smoked salmon strips or flaked salmon and pour in the cream, vodka and peas. Stir for 3–4 minutes until bubbling. Add the freshly ground black pepper to taste and return the pasta to the saucepan and lightly mix in the caviar.

Serve immediately on 4 plates and garnish with chopped chives.

PASTA WITH PESTO ALFREDO SAUCE

Serves 4

1 cup fresh basil leaves
1/2 cup pine nuts (or walnuts)
3 cloves garlic, crushed
1/4 cup olive oil
1 cup grated parmesan cheese
1 cup cream
500 grams approx. of pasta, farfalle, penne etc.
salt and freshly ground black pepper

In a food processor combine basil, pinenuts, garlic, olive oil and 1/2 cup of parmesan. Purée until smooth (this can be made up to 3–4 days ahead and stored in a sealed container in the fridge).

Cook pasta in a large saucepan of salted boiling water until tender and drain. Into the pasta saucepan pour the cream and bring to boil. Whisk in the basil pesto and season with salt and freshly ground black pepper. Return pasta to saucepan and toss with the cream sauce and the extra grated parmesan. Serve immediately garnished with shaved parmesan.

PASTA CARBONARA

Serves 4

Such an easy recipe for impromptu late-night instant suppers when you need food quick and it appears there's nothing prepared or in the fridge.

3–4 cups (approx.) of whatever pasta you have available (about 250 grams)
6 rashers of rindless bacon, or you can substitute slices of ham
1 tablespoon oil, or 25 grams butter
salt and freshly ground black pepper
Optional: a few button mushrooms, sliced (about 2 cups)
3 eggs beaten
1/4 cup chopped parsley
grated fresh parmesan cheese

Cook the pasta in lots of salted boiling water. While this is happening, using kitchen scissors, cut the bacon into little pieces. Drain the pasta. Heat oil or butter in the empty pasta saucepan and fry the bacon until crisp, 3–4 minutes. Add the mushrooms and stir-fry for 3 minutes then add lots of freshly ground black pepper (about 1/2 to 1 teaspoon). Return the pasta to the pan, remove pan from heat and pour in the beaten eggs and parsley, tossing to coat the pasta well with the egg. The heat of the pasta will cook the egg sufficiently. Don't return pan to heat or the egg will cook like scrambled egg. Divide into 4 dishes and top generously with fresh parmesan. Yum!

SEASONAL VEGETABLE PASTA PRESTO

Serves 4

450–500 grams stuffed fresh pasta (tortellini, ravioli etc., any flavour)
2 medium carrots, sliced
1 head of broccoli, broken into florets
1 cup frozen baby peas
2 cups (approx.) button mushrooms, sliced
1 red pepper, diced
2–3 zucchini, sliced
2 spring onions, sliced
8–12 black olives, pitted
2 teaspoons sweet chilli sauce
1/2 cup chopped parsley
1/2 cup approx. (150 ml pouch package or bottled) caesar salad dressing

Bring a large saucepan of salted water to the boil, add carrots and stuffed pasta and cook until almost tender. Add the broccoli and frozen peas, boil 2 more minutes and then add the mushrooms, capsicums and zucchini. Stir a further 1 minute then drain into a colander. Return pasta vegetable mix to the saucepan. Add the caesar dressing, olives, parsley and chilli sauce, toss and serve immediately.

PERFECT ROAST FILLET OF BEEF

Serves 4–6

*1 eye fillet of beef, trimmed of all sinew and fat and the same thickness throughout
(ask your butcher to cut it like this without any thin ends or scrappy pieces attached)
salt and freshly ground black pepper*

Preheat oven to 220°C. Place the meat in a roasting dish and season generously with salt and freshly ground black pepper. Place in the hot oven, quickly close the door so as not to let too much heat out. Time for exactly 20 minutes — not 19 and not 22, but bang on 20! When the timer buzzer goes off remove the roasting dish and cover meat with tinfoil (like a little tent). Rest the meat for 10–12 minutes like this before serving. This stops the meat 'bleeding' everywhere. The juices are brought to the meat's surface when it's cooking and resting it allows the juices to settle and soak back into the meat, keeping it tender and moist. The 20-minute rule always works for tender perfect pink but not bloody beef.

PERFECT PAN-ROASTED FILLET STEAKS

Pan-roasting is a simple technique that involves searing food on top of the stove, then completing the cooking in a hot oven. Pan-roasting gives a crisp crust and juicy interior to tender cuts of meat and poultry and thick pieces of fish.

*fillet steaks, sliced into 4–5cm thick pieces
(allow 1–2 per person depending on the appetite of big rugby-playing chaps
or more dainty eaters)*

Pan-fry over high heat to brown and sear the surface both sides of the steaks, then finish by placing the pan in a hot 220°C oven. (Make sure the handle is oven-proof.) Roast for 4 minutes for medium–rare, a little longer, say 5–6 minutes, for more well done. Remove from oven, cover pan with tinfoil like a tent and rest the meat 5–10 minutes to prevent bleeding of all the juices.

Sauces for Steak or Roast Fillet of Beef

SOUR CREAM GRAINY MUSTARD SAUCE

Serves 4–6

250 grams sour cream
3 tablespoons whole grain mustard
1 tablespoon chopped parsley
salt and freshly ground black pepper, to taste

Mix all ingredients, thoroughly seasoning to taste. Serve at room temperature over steaks or hot roast fillet of beef. Also great with grilled and barbecued chicken.

CRACKED PEPPERCORN CREAM CHEESE SAUCE

2 tablespoons oil
3 spring onions, finely sliced
1 clove garlic, crushed (1/2 teaspoon)
1 cup chicken or beef stock
125 grams approx. small wedge or round of cracked-pepper
creamy style cheese, cut into cubes

Heat oil in a small saucepan and add spring onions and garlic. Stir over medium heat for 3–4 minutes, add the stock and cubed cheese and stir for 2–3 minutes until cheese has melted and blended together into a thick sauce.

Perfect pan-roasted fillet steaks with sour cream grainy mustard sauce

HORSERADISH CHIVE CREAM SAUCE

250 grams sour cream
3 tablespoons prepared horseradish sauce
1/2 cup chopped chives and chive flowers

Mix all together until well combined and smooth. Serve at room temperature.

PEPPERCORN HORSERADISH & COGNAC SAUCE

2 cups beef stock
25 grams butter
4 spring onions, finely chopped
1 tablespoon green peppercorns in brine
1/2 cup red wine vinegar
2 tablespoons cognac
300 ml cream
2 tablespoons prepared horseradish sauce

Boil stock until it has reduced to 1/2 cup, about 15 minutes. Melt butter in a frypan over medium heat. Add spring onions and cook for 3–4 minutes until softened, then add drained peppercorns. Increase heat to high, add red wine vinegar and cognac and boil until liquid has reduced to 1/4 cup, about 4 minutes. Add reduced beef stock and cream. Boil, stirring, until reduced to a thick sauce consistency. Stir in horseradish sauce.

BABY MUSTARD MEATLOAVES

Serves 4

This is my mucked-about version of Lois Daish's original recipe for little tasty meatloaves wrapped and held together with rashers of bacon. They take meatloaf to a new culinary high and turn a rather ho-hum family meal into a dinner party delight.

800 grams minced lean beef
1 medium onion, finely chopped
3 cloves garlic, crushed (about 1 teaspoon)
1 tablespoon oil
1 1/2 cups fresh white breadcrumbs
2 eggs, beaten
salt and freshly ground black pepper, to taste
2 tablespoons grainy mustard
1 tablespoon tomato sauce
2 teaspoons sweet chilli sauce
1 tablespoon finely chopped parsley
1 tablespoon finely sliced chives
8 rashers rindless bacon

Heat oil in a small pan and stir fry onion until softened. Add garlic and breadcrumbs and cook 2 minutes. Mix mince with onion mixture then add beaten eggs, mustard, tomato and chilli sauces, parsley and chives. Season with salt and freshly ground black pepper. With wet hands form mince into 4 little meat loaves. Wrap 2 bacon rashers around each loaf and place in an oiled roasting dish. Bake in a preheated 190°C oven for about 30–35 minutes until the bacon is crisp and the meatloaves cooked right through.

These are splendid served with sour cream grainy mustard sauce (see page 82) and salad.

ORANGE SESAME BEEF
& BOK CHOY

Serves 4

250 grams mushrooms, sliced (about 3 cups)
4 spring onions, sliced (reserve a few green slices for garnish)
a large handful of thin asparagus, or green beans, trimmed and sliced
1 red pepper, sliced (or 1 chargrilled pepper)
1 head of broccoli, broken into small florets
3 medium carrots, cut into strips (or equivalent baby carrots)
2 tablespoons sesame oil
1 head of bok choy, chopped, about 2 cups
juice and grated rind of 1 orange
3 tablespoons oyster sauce
1 teaspoon sweet chilli sauce
1 tablespoon fresh ginger. grated
2 cloves garlic, crushed (1 teaspoon)
500 grams lean beef, thinly sliced into strips (no fat or sinew)

To garnish
1 tablespoon finely sliced green tops of spring onion
2 tablespoons toasted sesame seeds

Steam, boil or microwave all the vegetables except the bok choy until just tender, then refresh by plunging into cold water. Heat the sesame oil in a large frypan or wok, add the meat and stir-fry for 3–4 minutes until just cooked. You may need to do this in 2 batches. Remove meat, add the vegetables to the pan with the bok choy, orange juice and grated rind, oyster and sweet chilli sauce, ginger and garlic. Toss to heat through and mix well. Return the seared meat to the pan with the vegetables and toss 1–2 minutes to heat this through as well.

Serve on a large platter, sprinkle with toasted sesame seeds and the reserved finely sliced spring onion. Serve with rice.

SALMON CAKES WITH CITRUS HOLLANDAISE

Serves 4-6

4 large potatoes, peeled and cooked (dicing the potato speeds up the cooking)
3 cups approx. of flaked fresh cooked salmon (canned salmon also works well)
juice and grated rind of 1 juicy lemon
1 tablespoon sweet chilli sauce
salt and freshly ground black pepper
1/2 cup approx. finely chopped chives
1/2 cup flour
2 eggs
2 tablespoons milk
2 cups (approx.) dry toasted breadcrumbs

Thoroughly mash the potato then mix in the salmon, lemon juice and grated rind, sweet chilli sauce, salt and freshly ground black pepper and chives. Form into patties about 8 cm in diameter and dust with flour. Whisk milk and eggs together, dip salmon cakes into egg mixture then into breadcrumbs covering well. Chill for at least 1 hour. Fry in oil or clarified butter over medium heat until golden on both sides.

Serve with citrus hollandaise sauce (see next recipe).

FOOD-PROCESSOR
HOLLANDAISE SAUCE

4 egg yolks
2 tablespoons lemon juice
1 tablespoon white wine vinegar
salt and freshly ground black pepper
200 grams hot melted butter, plus 100 grams extremely
soft (just barely melted) butter

Place yolks in a blender or food processor and run machine. Slowly add lemon juice, white wine vinegar and salt and freshly ground black pepper. The yolks should be light, pale and creamy. Slowly drizzle in the hot melted butter then mix in the barely melted softened butter. Season to taste with salt and freshly ground black pepper.

Notes: Flavoured hollandaise sauces are easily produced using this method but by adding herbs, mustard substitutes and fresh fruit juices or flavoured vinegars.

For citrus hollandaise, replace lemon juice with 2 tablespoons fresh orange juice and 1/2 teaspoon finely grated rind.

SALMON NIÇOISE

Serves 4-6

2 handfuls whole baby green beans, topped and tailed
250 grams (10–12 approx.) tiny new potatoes
4 eggs, hardboiled
500 grams skinless salmon fillet, bones removed
1 glass approx. (200ml) white wine
2 tablespoons white wine vinegar
4 anchovy fillets, chopped
1/2 cup chopped mint
1/2 cup olive oil
1 telegraph cucumber, chopped
250 grams (2 cups approx.) small cherry tomatoes, cut in half
about 15 black olives, pitted
150 grams (3 handfuls) mixed salad leaves

Cook the beans in salted, boiling water 3–4 minutes and refresh by plunging them in cold water. Cook the potatoes in the boiling salted water for 10–12 minutes until just tender, drain and cool. Peel and quarter the hardboiled eggs. Place the salmon (cut fillet in half if need be) in a medium saucepan. Cover with the wine and white wine vinegar, season with salt and pepper then bring to the boil, cover and remove from heat. Leave salmon in liquid to cook as the liquid cools. Reserve the liquid and flake the salmon into chunky pieces. Mix in a small bowl the anchovies, mint and 4 tablespoons of the salmon liquid and the olive oil — season with salt and freshly ground black pepper. To serve, mix the beans, cucumber, cherry tomatoes, potatoes and olives with the salad leaves and dressing. Arrange on 4 individual plates and divide the salmon and eggs evenly on top of each portion.

BAKED SALMON FILLETS WITH A LEMON CHIVE SAUCE

Serves 4

Lemon Chive Sauce
1/4 cup sour cream
1/4 cup thick mayonnaise (Best Foods or homemade thick real mayonnaise)
1/4 cup chopped fresh chives
juice and grated rind of a lemon
1 teaspoon dijon style smooth mustard
salt and freshly ground black pepper, to taste

Salmon
4 salmon fillets, skin on but carefully remove any bones
(I find tweezers work well for this task)
salt and freshly ground black pepper

Sauce

Mix all ingredients together in a small bowl, season well with salt and freshly ground black pepper to taste. Cover and refrigerate (can be prepared one day ahead).

Salmon

Preheat oven to 200°C. Line a large baking sheet with tinfoil and spray with non- stick olive oil spray. Arrange salmon on foil, and spray them with olive oil and season with salt and freshly ground black pepper. Bake until just cooked through, about 15 minutes.

Transfer to serving plates and serve the sauce alongside. Garnish with chives and fresh chive flowers which are completely edible and add a snazzy splash of colour and texture.

Baked salmon fillets with a lemon chive sauce

CHICKEN WITH BROCCOLI & MUSHROOMS IN A BLACKBEAN SAUCE

Serves 4

1 head broccoli, broken into florets
250 grams button mushrooms, sliced (about 3 cups)
1 tablespoon sesame oil
1 tablespoon oil
2 onions, finely sliced
2 cloves garlic, crushed
2 tablespoons blackbean sauce, or to taste
1 tablespoon cornflour
1/4 cup water
1 handful of bean sprouts
1/4 cup chopped parsley or coriander
4 single, boneless, skinless chicken breasts, sliced into thin strips like french fries

Steam, boil or microwave broccoli florets until just tender and refresh by plunging in cold water. Heat oils in a large pan. Stir-fry chicken slices until browned and cooked through, about 3-4 minutes. Remove from pan, stir-fry onions until softened, add garlic, broccoli, mushrooms and black bean sauce. Return chicken to pan and toss to heat through. Mix cornflour with the water, add to pan and stir to mix well. Cook 2–3 minutes, seasoning to taste with salt and pepper. Pile onto a large platter and sprinkle with chopped parsley and bean sprouts. Serve with rice.

VEGES PASTA GRAINS & RICE

LENTIL BROWN RICE PILAU

Serves 4

This is great with a bowl of thick plain yoghurt passed separately as a sauce and is a perfect accompaniment to a tagine or meaty dish or as part of a vegetarian meal.

1 cup brown lentils
3 cups beef stock (or vegetable stock)
1 large onion
3 cloves garlic, crushed (1 teaspoon)
1 cup brown rice
3 tablespoons olive oil
1/2 teaspoon allspice
1 teaspoon ground cumin
salt and pepper
3 spring onions, finely sliced
1/2 cup (approx.) chopped parsley

Simmer brown lentils in the beef stock for 20 minutes. Roughly chop the onion and fry gently in the oil until golden brown. Add the garlic and rinsed brown rice, allspice and cumin and stir for 2 minutes. Add the lentils and stock and season with salt and pepper to taste. Stir well and bring to the boil. Reduce heat to very low and cover tightly. Cook (adding a little water if pilau is drying out too much) for 45 minutes, checking that the rice and lentils are tender. Stir through the sliced spring onions and parsley and serve.

GARLIC LEMON POTATOES

Serves 4

4 large Red Rascal potatoes, peeled if desired and cut lengthwise into 6 wedges
juice and grated rind of 2 lemons
200 grams melted butter
3 cloves garlic, crushed (1 teaspoon)
sea salt and freshly ground black pepper
2 tablespoons chopped parsley, to garnish

Preheat oven to 200°C. Combine potatoes with melted butter, lemon juice, crushed garlic, salt and freshly ground black pepper. Spread potatoes evenly in large baking dish and cook until tender and crispy golden brown, about 45 minutes. Sprinkle with chopped parsley to serve.

BASIC VINAIGRETTE SALAD DRESSING

3 tablespoons white wine or flavoured vinegar
(or half lemon juice half vinegar)
1/2 cup olive oil
1/2 teaspoon sugar
1 teaspoon prepared mustard
salt and freshly ground black pepper

Mix all together in a blender until well combined and emulsified.

This recipe can easily be doubled and keeps in a screw-top container in the fridge for at least a week.

CAULIFLOWER SWEET CHILLI SALAD

Serves 4–6

1 medium cauliflower, broken into small florets
3/4 cup oil
1 tablespoon sesame oil
4 tablespoons lemon juice
1 teaspoon grated lemon rind
2 sticks celery sliced finely
about 20 stuffed green olives, sliced
2 tablespoons capers, chopped
4 spring onions, finely sliced
1 tablespoon sweet chilli sauce
salt and freshly ground black pepper
1/2 cup chopped parsley
1/4 cup toasted sesame seeds

Bring a large saucepan of water to the boil and cook cauliflower in batches until just tender, about 5 minutes. Immediately refresh by plunging in cold water. In a blender mix oil, lemon juice and grated rind, salt and freshly ground black pepper and chilli sauce. Toss all ingredients together with the dressing and serve chilled.

RICE & BROCCOLI CHEESE MELT

Serves 4

A great way to have rice and vegetables all in one dish. You can always add some chicken to the ingredients and call it dinner.

2 heads of broccoli, broken into florets
2 spring onions, sliced
1 clove garlic, crushed
1 tablespoon oil
2 cups hot cooked rice (brown or white)
2 heaped tablespoons mayonnaise
1 tablespoon soy sauce
1 cup (approx.) grated cheese
2 slices fresh bread, made into breadcrumbs in the food processor

Preheat oven to 180°C. Microwave, boil or steam broccoli until just tender. Mix the broccoli, spring onion, crushed garlic, oil, rice, mayonnaise, soy and half the grated cheese together. Put the mix into a well-greased or sprayed lasagne type dish and sprinkle with the breadcrumbs and remaining grated cheese. Bake 25 minutes until cheese has melted and breadcrumbs are toasted golden brown.

LEMON STREUSEL GREEN BEANS

Serves 4

1 tablespoon olive oil
1/2 cup fresh white breadcrumbs
(whizz 2 slices toast bread in the food processor)
1 clove garlic, crushed (1/2 teaspoon)
1 teaspoon lemon pepper seasoning
2 big handfuls (500 grams) green beans, topped and tailed
juice and grated rind of 1 juicy lemon
50 grams butter or 1 tablespoon olive oil
1 tablespoon chopped parsley

Heat oil in a large pan over medium heat and sauté breadcrumbs, garlic and lemon pepper seasoning for about 5 minutes until crumbs are toasted and golden brown.

Microwave, boil or steam green beans until just tender and toss with butter or olive oil, lemon juice and grated rind. Sprinkle with the crumb mix and chopped parsley.

TEXAS STYLE POTATO SALAD WITH ROASTED CORN

Serves 4-6

6-8 medium red-skinned scrubbed potatoes — Red Rascals are excellent
2 cups whole kernel sweetcorn, fresh, frozen or canned is fine
olive oil spray
1/2 teaspoon chilli powder
1 cup mayonnaise, or mayonnaise style creamy dressing
1 teaspoon cajun seasoning
salt and freshly ground black pepper, to taste
juice and grated zest of 1 lemon
1/2 cup approx. chopped chargrilled pepper
(or use fresh red pepper)
1/2 cup chopped or sliced black olives, pitted
4 spring onions, finely sliced
1 cup roughly chopped parsley

Boil the potatoes in salted water for about 20 minutes until tender. Drain and cool to room temperature and cut into cubes. Spray a baking dish generously with olive oil, spread the corn in the dish in a single layer, liberally coat the corn with oil spray and sprinkle with chilli powder. Bake at 200°C for 15 minutes, occasionally stirring until roasted and slightly charred. Combine mayonnaise, cajun seasoning, salt and freshly ground black pepper, chargrilled, diced pepper, lemon juice and grated rind, olives, spring onions and parsley. Mix well then stir in the potato cubes, cover and refrigerate for at least 1 hour for flavours to develop.

Sprinkle with roasted corn and serve.

PARMESAN POLENTA

4 cups of well flavoured chicken or vegetable stock, or milk
1 1/2 cups polenta cornmeal
1 cup grated parmesan cheese
salt and pepper, to taste

Bring the stock or milk to the boil and add salt and pepper to taste. Pour the polenta into the boiling stock in a steady flow while you stir continuously. Turn down heat to a very gentle simmer for about 10 minutes. Stir until polenta is thick and smooth and pulls away from the edges of the saucepan. Stir in the parmesan cheese. The polenta can now be eaten in this basic form as an alternative to potatoes or pasta.

To fry polenta follow the method above but pour into a plastic wrap or foil-lined loaf or small cake tin and leave for an hour or so to set and cool. Slice into thick toast-like pieces and fry in hot oil for a few minutes until golden brown, or alternatively sprinkle slices with grated parmesan and grill on each side until a crisp brown crust forms. Serve with chunky tomato or mushroom sauce or pan-fried chicken livers and bacon.

CREAMY POTATO
& PASTA GRATIN

Serves 4

A good vegetable accompaniment to a main course or as a vegetarian main course.

2 cups potato, scrubbed and cubed into 1cm pieces
2 cups smallish dried pasta (macaroni or fusilli)
150 grams butter
3 medium onions, chopped
3 cloves garlic, crushed (1 teaspoon)
1 cup cream
1/2 cup milk
1 1/2 cups grated tasty cheese
1/2 cup grated parmesan cheese
salt and freshly ground black pepper

Boil the potato and pasta in the same water and when just tender, drain. Melt butter in a large pan and fry onion until softened, add garlic, cook for a further minute then pour in cream and milk and remove from heat. Stir cheese, potatoes, pasta, onion and cream together. Pour into a well-greased deep lasagne-type dish and bake 25–30 minutes in a 200°C oven until golden and crispy on top.

Feel free to add chopped ham, bacon, cooked chicken, smoked fish or prawns and any number of vegetables to this dish. It's a wonderful blueprint recipe that can be customised just by adding whatever is in season.

SIMPLE CRISPY ROAST POTATOES & ONIONS

Serves 4

Buying gourmet washed potatoes speeds up the process even further. Allow 2–3 small potatoes per person — people love these and I never seem to have leftovers.

12–16 small scrubbed potatoes
2 large onions
2–3 tablespoons extra virgin olive oil
a generous sprinkle of garlic salt
chopped parsley to garnish

Roughly chop potatoes into cubes or wedges — the smaller the pieces the quicker they cook. Peel and cut onions in quarters then eighths (like orange segments). Place potato and onions on a large shallow baking dish. Drizzle with olive oil and sprinkle with garlic salt, toss-ing to coat evenly. Bake in a hot oven 200°C until golden and crispy, about 20 minutes. Stir a couple of times. Sprinkle with chopped parsley to serve.

Simple crispy roast potatoes and onions

BUTTERED ONION & RICE CASSEROLE

Serves 4–6

An easy, full of flavour rice dish to accompany a main course. Don't be surprised at the unconventional cooking method. The large quantity of onions provide all the liquid necessary to plump up the rice. Don't put on your eye makeup before preparing this!

6 large onions, sliced
100 grams butter
2 cups long grain rice, brown or white
1/2 teaspoon salt
freshly ground black pepper
1/4 cup cream or milk
1 cup grated cheese
1/4 cup parsley chopped

Preheat oven to 150°C. Melt butter in a large oven-proof, flame-proof casserole. Stir in onions and coat well with butter.

If the rice is brown boil in a large saucepan of salted water for 5 minutes, to just soften the grains. Drain and add to the onions and season with salt and freshly ground black pepper. If using white rice just add to the onions and season with salt and freshly ground black pepper.

Cover and bake 3/4 of an hour (turn down heat to the lowest setting and hold for up to 3 hours at this stage). Before serving stir in the cream and grated cheese. Stir and serve sprinkled with chopped parsley.

BANANA CORIANDER SALAD

Serves 4

Just great to serve with chicken or barbecue grills or with hot spicy chilli dishes and curries.

2 cups sweetened natural yoghurt
(if using unsweetened add a little liquid honey to taste)
4 bananas cut into chunky slices
2 cloves garlic crushed (1 teaspoon)
1/2 cup coarsely shredded coconut
juice and grated rind of 1 juicy lemon
1 tablespoon sweet chilli sauce
1/2 cup chopped fresh coriander

Mix all ingredients together and chill.

KUMARA WITH RUM & RAISINS

Serves 4

4 large kumara, peeled and cut into 2 or 3 smaller pieces
50 grams butter
1/2 cup brown sugar
1/4 cup cream
1/4 cup rum
1/2 cup raisins
salt and freshly ground black pepper

Boil, steam or microwave kumara until just tender and place in a shallow small dish (small lasagne type). Melt butter in a small saucepan and over medium heat stir in brown sugar, cream and raisins and stir until sugar is dissolved. Pour over the kumara, season with salt and freshly ground black pepper and bake in a preheated 200°C oven for 25–30 minutes.

PAWPAW WATERMELON SALSA

Serves 4-6

This cool, colourful salsa is a delicious topper for grilled chicken and seafood. It's also perfect with whole fish cooked on the barbecue or as a side dish which just sings of summer. A smaller portion can be made if using as a salsa sauce not a salad. The fruit and coriander combination is so good.

1/2 an average-sized watermelon, peeled and chopped into small dice 1 cm square,
removing as many seeds as possible
1 pawpaw, peeled and seeded cut into similar size dice
1/2 small red onion or Pacific Sweet onion, finely chopped
1 tablespoon sweet chilli sauce
1/4 cup fresh squeezed lime or lemon juice and
1 teaspoon grated rind
2 tablespoons extra virgin olive oil
1/2 cup fresh coriander, chopped

Place all ingredients in a large bowl and toss to mix well. Season with salt and freshly ground black pepper and chill. Best eaten within 2 to 3 hours of making.

MUSHROOM HAZELNUT HONEY SALAD

Serves 4

5 tablespoons olive oil
1 tablespoon balsamic or red wine vinegar
2 tablespoons fresh tarragon, chopped
2 cloves garlic, crushed (1 teaspoon)
salt and freshly ground black pepper
1 tablespoon clear liquid honey
250 grams mixed mushrooms, sliced (about 3 cups)
(a mixture of buttons, flats, gourmet browns and fancy mushrooms like Shiitake)
4 handfuls of mixed baby lettuce
1/2 cup hazelnuts, toasted and chopped

Combine 4 tablespoons of the oil, vinegar, tarragon, garlic and honey in a small bowl and whisk until blended. Season with salt and freshly ground black pepper. Heat the remaining tablespoons of oil in a heavy frypan over medium heat, add the sliced mushrooms and sauté for 4–5 minutes. Add the hazelnuts and remove from heat. Toss lettuces with the dressing until the leaves are well coated. Divide among 4 salad plates and spoon mushroom and hazelnut mix over the salad.

PUDS & DESSERTS

GREEK COCONUT LEMON CAKE

125 grams butter
1 cup sugar
4 eggs
2 cups desiccated coconut
1 cup self-raising flour

Syrup
1 cup sugar
1/2 cup water
juice and grated rind of 2 lemons

In a food processor cream butter and sugar until light and fluffy, add eggs. Add coconut and flour, mix well and pour into a 20 cm square tin or loaf tin lined with baking paper. Bake in preheated oven at 200°C for 10 minutes then reduce heat to 150°C and bake a further 30 minutes or until cooked through when tested with a skewer. Stand for 5 minutes in the tin then pour the prepared syrup over. Cool completely in tin before removing.

Syrup

Place all ingredients in a small saucepan. Bring to boil, stir until sugar has dissolved. Reduce heat to simmer 5 minutes, then pour hot syrup over cake.

Serve warm with whipped cream as a dessert or in thin slices as an afternoon tea cake.

Greek coconut lemon cake with lemon curd

CHOCOLATE FUDGE BROWNIES

Makes about 15

This makes a fabulous base for a dessert, just add a scoop of ice-cream and Chocolate Fudge Sauce (see below). Garnish with strawberries or raspberries. Brownies can also be iced or frosted.

375 grams dark chocolate (or 1 packet chocolate melts)
200 grams butter
2 cups sugar
3 eggs
1 teaspoon vanilla essence
1 cup flour
1 cup chopped nuts, optional

Melt chocolate and butter together, stir until smooth and well blended. Mix in sugar, eggs and vanilla, then stir in flour and nuts. Pour into well-greased, approximately 20 x 30cm sponge roll tin. Bake at 180°C for 20–35 minutes or until a skewer inserted into the centre comes out with fudgy crumbs. Under, rather than overcook. The brownie should be quite fudgy and sticky, not dry and cake-like. Cool in the tin and cut into squares. Store in an airtight container.

CHOCOLATE FUDGE SAUCE

375 grams dark chocolate (or 1 packet chocolate melts)
300 ml cream

Place cream and chocolate in a saucepan and stir with a wire whisk over very gentle heat until the chocolate melts and is well combined with the cream. Cool for 30 minutes and then drizzle over brownies. Serve brownies with whipped cream and remaining sauce. It needs to be warmed to easily pour as it sets solid at room temperature.

CHOCOLATE CAMEO
MOUSSE CAKE

375 gram packet chocolate dark melts
2 cups cream
2 packets of cameo cream biscuits
extra whipped cream and shaved chocolate, to garnish

Grease and line the base of a 20 cm spring-form cake tin with paper. In a double boiler saucepan or easier still, the micro-wave, heat the chocolate and 1 cup of cream together until chocolate has melted. Stir until smooth and cool 5 minutes.

Place one packet of cameo creams in the food processor and finely crumb them. Add 2 tablespoons of the chocolate cream to moisten the crumbs further and press into the base of the springform cake tin. Whip the second cup of cream until soft peaks form. Gently fold cream and chocolate mixtures together. Pour approximately 1 cup of this over the biscuit crumb base. Break up or roughly chop the second packet of biscuits and sprinkle over a layer. Repeat with the chocolate cream then biscuit layer twice, finishing with a chocolate cream layer. Cover with plastic cling wrap and refrigerate at lease 12 hours (overnight). (Cake may be frozen at this stage, allow 4 hours to soften.)

To serve, run a thin hot knife blade around the edge of cake, slide tin carefully off and remove, lift cake off base and paper and position on a serving plate. Top each portion with a dollop of whipped cream and shaved chocolate.

RHUBARB SPICETRAIL
SHORTCAKE

A delicious 'homemade Mum's, kind of shortcake pud. Easy to make and always a winner for winter entertaining. Any leftovers are great with a cup of coffee the next day.

Base
125 grams butter
1/2 cup castor sugar
1 egg
1 1/2 cups self-raising flour

Topping
1/4 cup flour
2 cups castor sugar
4 sticks rhubarb, finely chopped
1 teaspoon mixed spice
2 eggs

Base
In food processor cream butter and sugar, add egg and self-raising flour. Press into baking paper-lined Swiss roll tin approximately 20 x 33 cm. Cover with topping and bake 55–60 minutes 180°C until firm and set. Dust with icing sugar and serve with cream.

Topping
Mix flour, sugar and eggs in food processor, add rhubarb and pulse until just combined. You don't want to over-process the chopped rhubarb.

Rhubarb can be substituted with raspberries, blackberries, gooseberries or feijoas, adjusting sweetening accordingly.

Rhubarb spicetrail shortcake

ESPRESSO CHOCOLATE MOUSSE

Makes 8–10 wineglass servings

This is very simple to make with only a couple of steps and no egg whites to beat and fold. It's very very rich and dense so a little goes a long way. I usually serve it in tiny demi-tasse coffee cups or small sherry or liqueur glasses with little coffee spoons (the sort you get from Great Granny in navy blue velvet-lined boxed sets for wedding presents). Fresh raspberries or sliced oranges are an excellent accompaniment or garnished with a little dollop of cream topped with a couple of chocolate-covered coffee beans.

375 grams dark chocolate (or 1 packet dark chocolate melts)
2 cups cream
3 tablespoons icing sugar
1 tablespoon of instant coffee (espresso) granules
1/4 cup liqueur or brandy (optional, I use Cointreau, Grand Marnier
or Baileys but just whatever you fancy)

Heat 1/2 cup cream and the coffee granules to dissolve. Either in the microwave or over very gentle heat in a small saucepan add the chocolate and stir until smooth. Beat the remaining 1 1/2 cups cream with the liqueur and icing sugar until thick and quite stiff. Fold a couple of tablespoons of cream into the chocolate mixture to thin it, then fold the chocolate mixture back into the remaining cream mixing until smooth.

Spoon the mousse into glasses or demi-tasse coffee cups and chill for at least 1 hour before serving.

BLUEBERRY YOGHURT FREEZE

1 cup thick plain natural yoghurt
2 tablespoons liquid honey
1/4 teaspoon (few drops) vanilla essence
1 punnet (approx. 1 1/2 cups) frozen blueberries

In a food processor combine yoghurt, honey and vanilla. Add frozen blueberries and pulse 4 or 5 times until combined but chunky. Test for sweetness, adding extra honey or icing sugar as required. Spoon into parfait glasses or small coffee cups. Serve immediately. Frozen raspberries can be substituted for blueberries.

FRENCH TOAST AS A DESSERT

A classic breakfast or brunch dish that works very well as a dessert. Dress up with lots of fresh fruit and garnish and no one will know it started life as a slice of day-old bread.

1/2 cup milk
1/2 cup castor sugar
3 eggs
1 teaspoon vanilla
1/2 teaspoon cinnamon
grated rind of 1 orange
6–8 thick slices diagonally cut french bread (day-old bread is best)
butter to fry in

In a food processor or blender, mix milk, castor sugar, eggs, vanilla and orange rind and pour into a shallow lasagne dish and dip in the slices of bread. Heat butter in a large frypan and fry both sides of bread until golden crispy brown. Dust with icing sugar and serve with sliced bananas or peaches, whipped cream and maple syrup or caramel sauce.

ORANGE LIQUEUR
SUGARPLUM TART

340 grams (2 cups approx.) plain or orange flavoured pitted prunes (1 packet
Sunsweet orange essence pitted prunes)
1/2 cup orange liqueur, Cointreau or Grand Marnier, or juice and grated rind of 1 orange
125 grams flour
600 ml milk
125 grams castor sugar
50 grams butter, melted
3 eggs

Soak prunes overnight or plump up in the microwave with the liqueur. In the bowl of a food processor, place flour, milk, castor sugar, melted butter, eggs and the orange liquid that the prunes have been soaking in. Run the machine until the mixture is a smooth batter.

Line a 23cm springform cake tin with tinfoil and spray with non-stick oil spray.

Cover the base with the prunes, pour batter over and bake at 160°C for 1 1/2 hours until the top is golden to dark brown and the filling set. If necessary, cover with tinfoil to prevent it overbrowning . Cool for 1/2 hour in the tin, then carefully undo the tin and remove the foil. Transfer the tart to a serving plate. Dust with icing sugar and serve with lightly whipped cream.

SUGAR-ROASTED FRESH FRUIT

Serves 4

An easy dessert of roasted/oven-poached fruit that can be dressed up to look extra special with vanilla icecream and mint sprigs. Almost any combination of fruit will work in this recipe.

1 cup blueberries
1 cup strawberries, halved
2 plums, pitted and roughly sliced
2 nectarines, pitted and roughly sliced
3 tablespoons castor sugar
1/2 teaspoon cinnamon
1/2 cup white wine, not too dry
vanilla icecream, to serve

Preheat oven to 180°C. Place fruit in a baking dish (a glass lasagne-style dish works well). Sprinkle with sugar and cinnamon then pour over the wine. Bake for about 45 minutes to an hour until the fruit is tender. Cool slightly and serve warm with vanilla icecream or softly whipped cream and fresh mint sprigs to garnish.

LITTLE APRICOT TARTS

Serves 4

1 packet flaky puff pastry sheets, thawed
6 ripe apricots
castor sugar

Cut out circles of pastry, roughly the size of small saucers (about 12 cm diameter). Place on a baking tray covered with non-stick baking paper. Preheat oven to 220°C and place an empty baking tray in the oven. Bring a deep saucepan of water to the boil and immerse the apricots, dunking them for 1 minute, then removing with a slotted spoon. Cut apricots in half, peel off the skins and remove stones. Place apricots flat side down on the rounds of chilled pastry, 3 halves to each. Generously dust with castor sugar and lift the baking paper up, transferring to the hot baking tray (the hot tray prevents soggy pastry bottoms). Bake for 15-18 minutes until puffed golden and crisp. Dust with icing sugar or extra castor sugar and serve warm with vanilla ice-cream or softly whipped cream.

Note: Plums, peaches and nectarines work equally as well, or you can substitute finely sliced peeled apples.

RED FRUIT CLAFOUTIS

Serves 4–6

Clafoutis is a French country classic. Traditionally it is made with cherries in a thick pancake-like batter, but I have developed one with a lighter custardy texture and you can use any sort of fruit. Wonderful with nectarines and peaches.

2 cups (approx.) fresh cherries halved and pitted
6 plums, quartered and pitted
juice and grated rind of a juicy orange
1/4 cup of castor sugar
3 tablespoons orange liqueur Cointreau or Grand Marnier
1 cup milk
1/2 cup flour
1/2 cup of sugar
3 large eggs
1 teaspoon vanilla essence
1/2 cup raspberries
1/2 teaspoon cinnamon

Mix cherries, plums, orange juice and grated rind, castor sugar and orange liqueur in a medium bowl and let stand for one hour. Preheat oven to 160°C (I use fan-bake). Arrange fruit mixture in a well-greased 6-cup baking dish (eg a small lasagne dish). In a food processor mix milk, flour, sugar, eggs and vanilla essence until well combined. Ladle over the fruit and scatter with the raspberries (these will sink into the batter) and sprinkle with cinnamon. Bake for 45–50 minutes until clafoutis is set in the centre. Dust with icing sugar and serve with lightly whipped cream.

ICED LEMON CHEESECAKE
WITH FRESH BERRY TOPPING

Makes large cheesecake to serve 6–8 people

To make the day before.

Base
4 x 250 gram containers of softened cream cheese
1 cup sugar
2 tablespoons orange liqueur (Grand Marnier or Cointreau
or freshly squeezed orange juice)
6 eggs
150 grams sour cream
juice and grated rind of 3 juicy lemons

Berry Topping
mixed berries
2 cups raspberries, blackberries, boysenberries, strawberries, blueberries etc.
2 tablespoons water
3 heaped tablespoons apricot jam

Preheat oven to 150°C, fan bake is best. Generously grease a 23 cm deep springform cake tin and line the base with baking paper. In a large bowl with an electric mixer beat cream cheese until light, smooth and creamy. Add orange liqueur and sugar and mix well. Add eggs one at a time beating well after each addition. Beat in sour cream, lemon juice and grated rind. Pour into prepared cake tin and bake approximately 1 1/2 hours.

The cheesecake should be set on the outside but still slightly wobbly in the centre. Cool in tin on wire rack, cover with plastic cling wrap and refrigerate overnight.

Run a small sharp knife around the tin to loosen sides, transfer to a cake plate and mound fresh berries over the top. Melt the jam and water over a gentle heat (or microwave) and pour or brush over the berries. Refrigerate, serve cut into wedges.

Iced lemon cheesecake with fresh berry topping

STRAWBERRY RHUBARB HAZELNUT CRISP

Serves 4–6 with generous seconds

Topping
1 1/2 cups flour
1 cup rolled oats
1 cup brown sugar
250 grams butter, cut into small pieces
1 cup chopped toasted hazelnuts

Fruit
4 large stalks fresh rhubarb,
sliced into 1 cm pieces
4 cups strawberries, roughly sliced
3/4 cup sugar, more or less, depending on tartness of rhubarb
1 tablespoon cornflour
2 tablespoons orange liqueur (Cointreau or Grand Marnier)

Mix flour, rolled oats, brown sugar and butter in a large bowl by hand, rubbing the butter in until the mixture clumps together. Mix in hazelnuts.

Preheat oven to 200°C. Mix the fruit, sugar, cornflour and liqueur together and place in a deep lasagne baking dish. Sprinkle topping over and bake for approximately an hour. The fruit bubbles up through the topping which bakes a golden, crispy brown. Cool slightly, dust with icing sugar and serve with whipped cream or icecream.

SOUR CREAM CINNAMON
PEACH CAKE

A great dessert cake that will have them lining up for seconds. Nectarines, peeled apple, raw rhubarb, blackberries etc. can be substituted for peach.

Cake
3 cups chopped peeled fresh peaches
100 grams butter softened
3 cups brown sugar, loosely packed
2 eggs
250 grams sour cream
1 teaspoon vanilla essence
2 cups flour
1 teaspoon baking soda
1/2 teaspoon salt
1 teaspoon cinnamon

Topping
1 cup brown sugar
2 teaspoons cinnamon

In a food processor mix butter and sugar until creamy, add eggs, sour cream and vanilla essence then add flour, baking soda, salt and cinnamon. Add peaches and pulse the machine just a couple of times to lightly mix in the fresh peach — don't overprocess. Pour mixture into a well greased 20–23cm loose-bottomed springform tin with the base lined with baking paper.

Mix the topping, brown sugar and cinnamon together and sprinkle through a coarse sieve evenly over the cake. Bake at 180°C for 1 1/4 hours and cool in the tin. When cold carefully remove the sides of tin and ease off the bottom lining paper. Serve the cake warm with lightly whipped cream or thick yoghurt.

BUTTERSCOTCH MERINGUES

Makes a large platter of piled up meringues, enough to feed at least 6–8 generously. The recipe halves easily.

6 egg whites (room temperature)
2 cups castor sugar
1 teaspoon butterscotch or caramel essence (you can substitute vanilla;
I use Watkins Butternut essence which is absolutely delicious
and a very good 'secret' ingredient — an intense butterscotch flavour)
1 teaspoon malt vinegar
2 teaspoons cornflour
whipped cream, to serve

In a large metal, porcelain or glass (ie not plastic) bowl beat egg whites until soft peaks form. A hand-held electric beater is ideal for this job. Gradually, a teaspoon at a time, add the castor sugar. I emphasise, add the sugar slowly. The mixture should be getting glossy, thick and shiny with each addition and the whole sugar-adding process should take at least 10 minutes. Beat in the essence, vinegar and cornflour. Spoon mixture out into little 'blobs' onto a baking paper-covered baking tray. Bake in a low 110–120°C oven for approximately 45 minutes until dry and crisp. The meringues should just lift off the paper easily. Cool on a wire rack and jam together with whipped cream when cold.

This is a wonderful pavlova recipe if you make it into one large plate-size mound on the baking tray. Cooking time will be a little longer, but bake at the same temperature (110–120°C) for about 1 1/2 hours.

Butterscotch meringues

STRAWBERRY FOOL

Serves 4

Incredibly simple but delicious pud made in a jiffy — but one your guests will think has taken hours. This recipe works equally well with raspberries, blackberries, boysenberries etc. Adjust the amount of sugar to taste, depending on tartness of berries.

2 cups (approx.) ripe strawberries, hulled and roughly chopped
2 tablespoons castor sugar
2 tablespoons orange liqueur (Grand Marnier or Cointreau)
300 mls cream

Mash strawberries, liqueur and sugar with a fork — don't overwork as you want to mash not purée the fruit. Leave 15–20 minutes. Whip the cream until soft peaks form, not too stiff. Fold in the mashed strawberries and spoon into tall wine or parfait glasses. Refrigerate at least 2 hours before serving.

ALMOND TULIP BASKETS

Makes 4–6

100 grams butter, softened
3/4 cup castor sugar
3/4 cup flour
3 egg whites
1/2 cup finely ground almonds

In a food processor mix butter, castor sugar, flour and egg whites. When the sugar is well beaten in and dissolved add the almonds then chill the mixture. On a non-stick baking tray or a baking tray covered with a sheet of baking paper flatten out spoonfuls of mixture to 15 cm, saucer-shaped discs. Bake at 180°C for 8–10 minutes until pale golden. Cool for about 1 minute on the tray then carefully lift off and shape over small cup-sized dishes to cool completely. Fill with icecream and fresh fruit or sorbet, fool or mousse. These store a couple of days in an airtight container but are best made fresh on the day.

IMPOSSIBLE PIE

Serves 6

Impossible Not! The beauty of this recipe is you throw all ingredients in the food processor, whizz for few moments then pour into a pie/flan dish and hey presto, it separates into a self-crusting coconut creamy pie, quick and easy.

100 grams butter, softened
1 cup sugar
4 eggs
1/2 cup flour
2 cups milk
2 teaspoons vanilla essence, or
(optional) a good slosh — ie 3 tablespoons — Baileys Irish Cream liqueur
1 cup desiccated coconut

In a food processor mix butter and sugar until creamy, add eggs, then all other ingredients. Mix until a smooth batter. Pour into a greased, 23 cm pie or flan dish. Bake at 180°C for 1 hour until the top springs back when lightly touched.

Serve warm, dusted with icing sugar.

Icecream

I love icecream desserts and have found an icecream maker one of my most-used kitchen gadgets. It's definitely not an extravagance, as it's such a versatile machine. It produces sublime frozen margaritas, gin and tonic sorbets and chilled, slushy, iced Bloody Marys plus, of course, icecream and sorbets. My machine makes the stuff in under half an hour so it's almost a between-course procedure, although it's so easy to make a decent batch and have it in the freezer on standby for dinner parties. So many of my food memories are icecream-related, from the first thing you were allowed to eat after having your tonsils out to that most desired treat that ex-pat Kiwis yearn for all around the world — hokey-pokey icecream in a cone or a Jelly Tip.

Presentation is all-important with icecream. Really rich flavours are best in tiny portions, perhaps with a splash of liqueur poured over them in a wine or sherry glass. I find my collection of silver christening mugs or even demi-tasse coffee cups great for icecream desserts. Big parfait glasses and old-fashioned stemmed coupe dishes look great when laden with fruits and icecream and masses of mint garnish — and don't forget almond tulip cups, brandy snap baskets and cones!

If you haven't got a machine or the time and inclination to make your own icecream, buy top quality vanilla icecream and go from there, stirring in the flavourings and refreezing. Even some fruit jams or conserves, Christmas mincemeat, marmalade or crushed gingernut biscuits or brandy snaps can make great impromptu icecream dreams.

SIMPLE ICECREAM BASE

Serves 4

1 carton of custard (600ml pack)
300 ml cream, lightly whipped (or thick yoghurt)
150 ml milk

Stir all ingredients together in a bowl with a wire whisk or electric mixer. Add flavourings and pour into an icecream machine. Freeze according to the manufacturer's instructions.

To the make the icecream base from scratch
3 eggs
1 cup castor sugar
600 ml cream
150 ml milk

Whisk egg yolks and sugar until pale and fluffy, about 3 minutes. Either microwave mixture for 1 minute on high then whisk again, or whisk over a bowl of hot water for a few minutes to dissolve the sugar. Stir in the cream and milk and blend well, add flavourings of your choice and pour into an icecream machine. Freeze according to manufacturer's instructions.

CAPPUCCINO FOAM WITH WALNUTS

Add:

1/2 cup strong espresso
1/2 cup icing sugar
3 tablespoons Kahlua or coffee liqueur
1 cup walnut halves, toasted

PEACHY VANILLA

Add:

2 cups peach purée, either fresh, peeled or canned
1 cup finely chopped peach pieces
2 teaspoons vanilla essence
1/2 cup icing sugar
1/2 teaspoon ground cinnamon

STRAWBERRY PEPPER CRUSH

Add:

2 cups approx. strawberry purée
1/2 teaspoon finely ground pepper
(this really brings out the strawberry flavour)
1–2 teaspoons strawberry essence
1/2 cup icing sugar

LEMON CURD & GINGER

Add:

1 1/2 cups lemon curd
6–8 pieces crystallised ginger, finely chopped

DOUBLE VANILLA CINNAMON CREAM

Add:

2 teaspoons extra strength vanilla essence
150 grams sour cream, beaten with
1 cup loosely packed soft brown sugar
1 teaspoon ground cinnamon

BAILEYS TOASTED COCONUT

Add:

1 cup toasted coarsely shredded coconut
1 teaspoon coconut essence
1/2 cup Baileys liqueur

BUTTER PECAN FUDGE

Add:

1 can sweetened condensed milk, caramelised (see page 135)
Melt 50 grams butter in a large pan.
Stir-fry 1 cup pecans in butter until golden brown, 2–3 minutes.

'J.D.' (JACK DANIEL'S) BANANA SPICE

Add:

3 bananas, puréed
1 teaspoon mixed spice
1 teaspoon vanilla
1 cup loosely packed brown sugar
1/4 cup Jack Daniel's bourbon

Icecream Sauces

BOURBON–BUTTER SAUCE

For icecream, especially fudge or coffee icecream

3 tablespoons light corn syrup or liquid glucose
(available in supermarkets, delis and some chemists)
1 teaspoon fresh lemon juice
1 cup sugar
125 grams butter
3 tablespoons bourbon
1 teaspoon butterscotch or vanilla essence

Place corn syrup, lemon juice, sugar and 2 tablespoons of water in a small non-stick saucepan. Stir over medium heat until the sugar is dissolved. Bring to the boil and watch carefully as it boils and changes to a golden caramel colour. Don't stir, just swirl the saucepan around gently and watch as it changes quickly, should take 5–6 minutes. Remove from heat and stir in the butter, then essence and bourbon. Cool slightly then pour over icecream.

RASPBERRY LEMON SAUCE

125 grams butter
1/2 cup castor sugar
juice and grated rind of 1 juicy lemon
1 1/2 cups approx. (1 punnet) of raspberries, reserve a few for garnish
1/4 cup water

Melt butter in a non-stick frypan. Stir in sugar, lemon juice, lemon rind and 1/4 cup water. Stir over gentle heat until sugar is dissolved. Stir in the raspberries and mash with a fork. Stir until the sauce thickens then pour over icecream using reserved raspberries as garnish. (Blueberries, blackberries etc. can replace raspberries; adjust the sugar accordingly.)

STRAWBERRY BALSAMIC SAUCE

125 grams butter
1/2 cup brown sugar
3 cups chopped strawberries, plus a few reserved for garnish
2 teaspoons balsamic vinegar

Melt butter in a large non-stick frypan. Add brown sugar and stir until sugar dissolves. Add balsamic vinegar and strawberries. Stir until strawberries release their juices. Cool slightly and serve over icecream with whole reserved strawberries as garnish.

CHOCOLATE FUDGE SAUCE

375 grams dark chocolate (1 packet dark chocolate melts)
300 ml cream
shaved or chopped chocolate, to decorate

Place cream and chocolate in a saucepan and stir with a wire whisk over very gentle heat, until the chocolate melts and is well combined with the cream. Pour over icecream and decorate with shaved or chopped chocolate. (Serve the sauce while still warm as it sets solid at room temperature.)

DEAD EASY CONDENSED MILK CARAMEL SAUCE

1 x 400 gram can sweetened condensed milk

Place can with label removed in a deep small saucepan and cover with water. Bring to the boil then gently simmer for 2 hours. Cool slightly before opening and hey presto, a gorgeous, rich, caramel fudge sauce. This is great mixed with whipped cream as a filling for cakes and meringues, in icecream or over a pavlova.

BUTTERSCOTCH SAUCE

125 grams butter
1 cup brown sugar
1 cup cream
1 teaspoon cornflour
1 tablespoon cold water
1 teaspoon vanilla essence

Place butter, sugar and cream in a small heavy saucepan. Stir over low heat until brown sugar dissolves and butter melts. Add cornflour mixed with cold water. Increase heat and bring to boil. Stir in vanilla and cool. Cover and refrigerate, keeps up to a week. Warm to serve.

SPEEDY TIRAMISU DESSERT PARFAITS

Serves 4

3 tablespoons castor sugar
2 tablespoons boiling water
1 tablespoon good quality instant coffee powder
3/4 cup Kahlua or other coffee liqueur
300 ml cream, lightly whipped
250 grams cream cheese, softened
8 slices (approx. 2cm thick) of plain madeira or sponge cake
2 teaspoons cocoa

In a food processor combine sugar, boiling water and instant coffee powder mix until sugar is dissolved. Add Kahlua and soft cream cheese and mix until smooth. Add whipped cream and quickly mix to combine. Place 1 slice of cake in the bottom of each of the 4 parfait or wine glasses. Spoon in half the Kahlua cream mixture then cover with another slice of cake, breaking cake if necessary to fit in the glasses. Add the remaining Kahlua cream mixture and dust with cocoa. Refrigerate for at least 1 hour and up to 6 hours.

FRESH BAY POACHED PEARS

Serves 4

4 pears, firm not overripe, peeled but with stems still attached
2 glasses of red wine, a full-bodied cabernet is best
1 cup sugar
6 fresh bay leaves
1 vanilla bean
2 cups cold water (approx.)

In a deep saucepan big enough to hold the 4 pears place red wine, sugar, bay leaves and vanilla bean and stir over medium heat to dissolve sugar. Place the peeled pears in the wine mix and add water to cover. Gently simmer the pears until tender, about 40 minutes. Watch the poaching liquid doesn't evaporate too much. Add more water (or wine) to keep the pears covered. When tender carefully remove pears (don't lift out with the now fragile stem but use a slotted spoon). Place on a plate while you vigorously boil the poaching liquid to reduce to a thick syrupy consistency, removing bay leaves and vanilla bean. Serve pears on plate with a dollop of whipped cream and the syrup poured over. Garnish with fresh bay leaves or mint.

Alternatively for an extra special glamour dessert, pour melted chocolate over the pears and serve with the syrup sauce and cream on the side. This looks pretty spectacular for a special occasion.

CHOCOLATE SURPRISE PISTACHIO KISSES

Serves 4

1 sheet frozen flaky puff pastry, thawed
2 Mars bars, or other chocolate bars of your choice, or even plain chocolate chips
1/4 cup (approx.) pistachio nuts
icing sugar, for sprinkling
optional extras: a few raspberries or strawberries and mint sprigs, to garnish

Further roll out the sheet of pastry to measure approximately 28 x 28 cm and cut into 4 equal squares approximately 7 x 7cm. With a large sharp knife chop up the Mars bars into tiny pieces about the size of an olive. Divide the chopped Mars bars and pistachio nuts into 4 and spoon in the centre of each small square of pastry. Bring pastry corners together just above the filling, twist and turn into a little pouch. Fan out the corners. Place on a baking sheet and bake in a preheated 200°C oven for 15–20 minutes until puffed and golden brown. Let stand for a further 10 minutes to help the melting process. Sprinkle with icing sugar and serve with whipped cream and garnish as desired with fresh fruit and mint sprigs.

Note
Double layered and buttered phyllo pastry also works well with this recipe.

Chocolate surprise pistachio kisses

INDIVIDUAL APPLE & BLACKBERRY PIES WITH STREUSEL CRUMBLE

Serves 4

1 or 2 sheets (depending on muffin tin size) of frozen flaky puff pastry, thawed
1 cup thickly stewed apple (microwaved without extra water, or
alternatively use canned apple pie filling)
1 cup approx. blackberries fresh or frozen (or raspberries, blueberries)
sugar to taste, about 1/4 cup
1/2 teaspoon cinnamon

Streusel Crumble
50 grams butter
1/2 cup flour
1/4 cup sugar
1 tablespoon rolled oats

Cut out squares of pastry to line non-stick regular or larger Texas-size muffin tins. Push the pastry down into the base of the tins — the corners stick up above the rim. Mix the apple, blackberries, cinnamon and sugar together and spoon into the pastry-lined tins.

In a food processor mix the streusel crumble ingredients together to form a coarse crumbly mixture. Sprinkle the topping loosely over the apple in the muffin tins and bake in a preheated 180°C oven until pastry is puffed and crisp and the topping golden and crumbly — approximately 20 minutes. Remove pies from the tins while still warm and dust with icing sugar. Serve with lightly whipped cream or icecream.

'BLAST FROM THE PAST' CHOCOLATE FUDGE PUD

An old-fashioned dead easy pud when you appear to have nothing in the cupboard or fridge. This can be whizzed up in a flash and is really quite impressive with its dark, fudgy, chocolate sauce layer under a steamed pudding-like spongy topping. A splash of orange liqueur in with the boiling water is a smart touch when you want to go overboard with the impressive part and the recipe can be divided up into individual pudding servings made in small ramekins or soufflé dishes.

Sponge Layer
1/2 cup milk
3/4 cup sugar
2 teaspoons baking powder
50 grams melted butter
1 cup flour
1/4 teaspoon salt

Sauce Layer
1/2 cup sugar
2 tablespoons cocoa
1 3/4 cups boiling water

For the sponge layer, place all ingredients in a food processor and mix until smooth and well combined. Pour into a lasagne dish approx. 25 x 20 cm.

For the sauce layer, mix the sugar and cocoa and sprinkle over the top of the sponge mixture. Carefully pour the boiling water to cover the cocoa and sugar topping. Bake at 180°C for 40 minutes until well-risen and cake-like on top. Dust with icing sugar and serve with icecream and/or whipped cream.

CHOCOLATE SORBET

2 heaped tablespoons cocoa
2 cups water
200 grams dark chocolate
1 cup sugar

Place cocoa, sugar and water in a saucepan and stir over medium heat until sugar is dissolved. Add the chocolate and stir until melted. Chill, then freeze in an icecream machine following manufacturer's instructions.

Serve in parfait glasses garnished with shaved chocolate and a little cream.

FROZEN PEACH SCHNAPPS BELLINIS

Serves 4

3 large ripe peaches
1 tablespoon lemon juice
3 tablespoons peach schnapps (or Cointreau)
3 egg whites
1/2 cup castor sugar
300 ml cream, whipped

Plunge the peaches into boiling water for 1 minute, remove and rub off the skin, slice the flesh into a blender and purée with the lemon juice and peach schnapps. Whisk the egg whites until foamy then slowly add the castor sugar a teaspoon at a time until the mixture reaches a smooth glossy meringue consistency. Fold the peach purée, egg whites and whipped cream together and pour into a foil-lined loaf tin. Freeze solid for at least 6 hours, preferably overnight.

To serve, slice the frozen peach loaf and serve with fresh peach slices and peach purée as a sauce (to make this, prepare a second batch of the peaches, lemon juice and peach schnapps).

CARAMELISED RASPBERRY BRÛLÉE

Serves 4

2 punnets (approx. 3 1/2 cups) fresh ripe raspberries
4 tablespoons raspberry liqueur, or liqueur of your choice
(the orange-flavoured ones are particularly good, Cointreau or Grand Marnier)
250 grams cream cheese, softened
1 cup cream, lightly whipped
1/2 cup icing sugar
1/2 cup (approx.) castor sugar

Divide the raspberries between 4 ovenproof small soufflé dishes or ramekins, reserving a few perfect ones for garnish. Sprinkle with liqueur and a little sugar if desired depending on sweetness of berries. Beat the cream cheese, cream and icing sugar together until smooth. Divide and spread this over the raspberries in the 4 individual dishes. Chill for at least 2 hours and up to 24 hours. When ready to serve, sprinkle the top of each dish liberally with the castor sugar, making sure the whole surface is well covered. Use a little extra castor sugar if required. Place the dishes under a preheated grill and cook for a couple of minutes until the surface bubbles and turns a golden caramel colour. Serve with a few extra raspberries to garnish.

Ripe apricots, peaches and strawberries are just as delicious used in this recipe.

RED WINE & CINNAMON SORBET

Serves 4

Sorbets are perfect, light, summery desserts. Best served in wine or liqueur glasses in small portions, have the sorbet out at room temperature for 10 minutes to soften before serving.

2 1/4 cups red wine
1 1/4 cups water
3/4 cup sugar
4 cinnamon sticks

Heat in a large saucepan, stirring until the sugar is dissolved. Bring to the boil, then turn off heat and cool for 45 minutes. Strain out cinnamon sticks and freeze in an icecream machine following manufacturer's instructions.

RASPBERRY PEACH SORBET

Serves 4–6

2 cups sugar
2 cups water
3 ripe peaches, peeled and chopped
1 punnet (approx. 1 1/2 cups) raspberries
juice and rind of 1 juicy lemon

Dissolve the sugar in the water, stirring over medium heat. Purée the peaches and raspberries using the sugar syrup to thin the mixture. Add the lemon juice and grated rind. Pass the mixture through a sieve to remove any raspberry pips and coarse fibres. Chill then freeze in an icecream machine following the manufacturer's instructions.

BAKING & TREATS

FOCACCIA BREAD

The food-processor variety

1 tablespoon dried yeast granules
1 1/2 cups warm water
1/2 teaspoon sugar
4 1/2 cups flour
1/2 cup olive oil
1 teaspoon salt
rock or sea salt
rosemary

In food processor mix yeast, water and sugar. When frothy, add flour, oil and salt. Run machine until dough is smooth and non sticky. Place in oiled bowl covered with plastic cling wrap. Leave to rise until doubled in bulk, approximately 1 hour.

Knead on floured bench and flatten in a well-oiled roasting dish to 2cm thick. Cover and rise again until doubled in size. Make indentations in the top with fingertips and drizzle with oil, sprinkle with salt and rosemary as desired. Bake at 220°C for 15 minutes then reduce heat to 200°C. Cook for further 25–30 minutes and cool.

Round and square focaccia bread (the food-processor variety)

SCONES

The lemonade method for ultra quick scones in a jiff. I've even served these with fresh strawberries for dessert.

4 cups self-raising flour
300 ml cream (1 carton or small bottle of cream)
1 can lemonade (355 ml)
1/2 teaspoon salt

Mix all ingredients in a bowl to a smooth dough. Tip out onto a well-floured surface and cut into squares or press out with a scone cutter. Bake at 220°C (fan-bake if you have it) for about 15–20 minutes until starting to colour golden. Check they are cooked through and cool on a wire rack.

Serve warm with jam or whole fruit pre-serves and whipped cream, garnish with fresh fruit as desired.

BEER BREAD

Makes 1 large loaf 20 x 10 cm or 2 smaller loaves

A wonderful 'quick bread' that has the texture and taste of a farmhouse loaf, gorgeous, yeasty smells and made in a jiffy without all that planning for hours, bowls of dough rising in the hotwater cupboard, kneading and fiddling about. You don't even have to take off your rings to make this one.

This bread can be made with a variety of flours, wholemeal and mixed grain, etc. Allow 1 teaspoon baking powder per cup of flour — and of course it can be topped with other things besides cheese, such as sesame seeds, rosemary, flaked sea salt, paprika and poppy seeds. A great idea is to make a stuffed bread using this basic recipe. Place half the mixture in the loaf tin. Spoon in a layer of onion marmalade (see page 14) and perhaps a layer of chargrilled peppers, spinach leaves, pitted olives. Spoon in the remaining dough and bake as per directions.

3 cups flour
3 teaspoons baking powder
1 teaspoon salt
1 can beer (made up to 500 ml with water)
1 handful grated cheese

Preheat oven to 200°C. Quickly mix all ingredients together and spoon into a greased or non-stick loaf tin and top with grated cheese. A large 20 x 10 cm loaf tin will take 1 hour but smaller tins 8 x 15cm take 35–40 minutes.

WHOLEMEAL BROWN SODA BREAD

Makes 1 medium cob loaf

2 1/2 cups flour
1 3/4 cups wholemeal flour
1 teaspoon baking soda
1 teaspoon baking powder
1 teaspoon salt
50 grams butter
500 ml buttermilk
(or substitute 500 ml milk mixed with 2 tablespoons malt vinegar)

Mix all ingredients together in a food processor. Turn out onto a floured surface. Form into a rounded cob shape and place on a well-greased oven tray. Score the top surface in a criss-cross pattern with a knife. Bake in a preheated 200°C oven for 20 minutes then turn down oven temperature to 180°C and bake for further 25–30 minutes. Cool to room temperature on a wire rack before slicing with a serrated bread knife. This can also be made in a large loaf tin but remember to grease it really well first.

Beer bread in foreground with wholemeal brown soda loaf behind

'COUNTRY PARISH' CHEESE BREAD

Serves 4–6

A handy lunchtime bread that takes no time to whisk together and cook. It may be called Country Parish because my other quick bread contains beer. A quick bread is one without yeast and without having to think about it the day before, and with the vicar doing his rounds one could never be too sure whether beer would be acceptable. Anyway, it's an old farming family recipe from way back and has always been known as Country Parish Bread so I'm sticking with that!

4 cups flour
2 tablespoons sugar
1 tablespoon baking powder
1 1/2 teaspoons salt
125 grams butter, cut into small pieces
4 cups grated cheddar or tasty cheese
1 tablespoon chopped dill (or finely chopped chives)
2 cups milk
2 eggs

Preheat the oven to 200°C. Grease 2 medium loaf tins well. Place flour, sugar, baking powder and salt in the food processor. Add the butter and run machine until the mixture resembles breadcrumbs. Add the cheese and dill, quickly mix in the eggs and milk. Don't overmix. Divide the dough into the 2 tins and bake for approximately 40–45 minutes until bread is well risen and golden brown on top and feels hollow when tapped. Remove from oven and allow to cool in the tin for 10 minutes before tipping out on a wire rack to cool completely.

MICROWAVE BUTTERNUT BRITTLE

Speedy and quick for a treat with coffee or as a foodie gift.

1 1/2 cups dry roasted peanuts
1 cup sugar
1/2 cup light corn syrup or liquid glucose
(available at delis and some chemists)
1/4 teaspoon salt
50 grams butter
1 teaspoon vanilla essence
1 heaped teaspoon baking soda

Place a sheet of baking paper on an oven tray and spray with non-stick oil spray. In a large microwave proof bowl combine peanuts, sugar, corn syrup and salt. Cook on high until mixture bubbles vigorously, about 5 minutes and stir in the butter and vanilla essence. Return to microwave and cook on high a further 3–4 minutes until the mixture turns a golden colour. Working quickly stir in the baking soda and blend well — the mixture will foam up. Immediately pour out onto the prepared baking paper and tilt tray to spread evenly. Cool then break into pieces and store in airtight container at room temperature.

DARK CHOCOLATE FUDGE

An easy after-dinner treat to have with coffee or to make as a gift. It always works and is fairly quick to prepare, although it needs to be well chilled to cut up into pieces.

200 grams marshmallows (1 large packet)
100 grams butter
1 tablespoon water
375 grams dark chocolate (1 packet chocolate melts)
1 teaspoon vanilla essence
1 cup nuts (pecans, walnuts etc.)
Optional extras: chocolate raisins, broken hokey pokey pieces,
miniature marshmallows, tiny sweeties, jellybeans

Place marshmallows, butter and water in a large microwave proof bowl and microwave on high for 3 minutes, stirring once or twice as marshmallows and butter melts. Stir in the chocolate, cook in bursts of 30 seconds on high, stirring to blend melted chocolate into marshmallows. Add vanilla essence and mix to combine well. Add nuts and any optional extra bits and pieces. Turn out into a tinfoil-lined 20 cm square cake tin and chill. Chill for at least 2 hours but preferably overnight then slice into pieces and store in the fridge.

Top: Dark chocolate fudge. Bottom: Microwave butternut brittle (page 153)

OVER THE TOP CHOCOLATE CHIP NUTS & BOLTS COOKIES

Dentist's revenge!

2 1/2 cups rolled oats
1 cup chocolate chips
500 grams butter, softened
1 cup brown sugar
1 cup white sugar
2 eggs
2 teaspoons vanilla
2 cups flour
1/2 teaspoon salt
1 teaspoon baking powder
1 teaspoon baking soda
1 cup dark chocolate chips or chocolate pieces
1 cup white chocolate chips or chocolate pieces
1/2 cup mixed chopped roasted walnuts, pecans and skinned hazelnuts

In a food processor mix the first cup of chocolate chips and the rolled oats. Run machine until this is finely ground, and set aside.

Beat butter, brown and white sugar in food processor until creamy, add eggs and vanilla. Add flour, salt, baking powder and baking soda. Mix in the chocolate chips, nuts and oatmeal mixture but don't over process these last 3 ingredients; just quickly incorporate them into the mixture. Place large dessertspoons of mixture on a non-stick or paper-lined baking tray and press down, leaving plenty of room for spreading.

Bake 12–15 minutes in 200°C oven. Cookies will appear slightly underdone (soft in the centre). Allow to rest on the tray for a couple of minutes then transfer to a wire rack to cool.

'HAPPY BIRTHDAY' LARGE DEEP CELEBRATION CHOCOLATE CAKE

1 3/4 cups flour
2 cups sugar
3/4 cup cocoa
2 teaspoons baking soda
1 teaspoon baking powder
1 teaspoon salt
2 eggs
2 teaspoons vanilla essence
1 cup strong black coffee (espresso)
1 cup buttermilk, or milk
1/2 cup soya oil

Mix everything in a food processor until smooth and well combined. Pour into a greased and baking paper-lined cake tin 23–25cm. Bake at 180°C for approximately 1 1/2 hours. (Test that a skewer inserted in the centre of the cake comes out clean with no gooey cake mixture still clinging to it.) Cool on a wire rack and ice when completely cold.

Chocolate Icing
125 grams butter, softened
1 cup dark chocolate chips, melted
3 1/2 cups icing sugar
1/4 cup milk
1 teaspoon vanilla essence

In a large bowl with an electric mixer, beat butter until soft and creamy. Add melted chocolate, icing sugar, milk and vanilla essence. Beat until icing is smooth and spreadable.

APPLE CIDER COCONUT CAKE

1 cup apple juice or cider, heated until nearly boiling
200 grams (1 cup) dates, coarsely chopped
1 teaspoon baking soda
125 grams butter
1 1/2 cups castor sugar
2 eggs
1 teaspoon vanilla
1 1/2 cups flour
2 large apples, peeled, cored and chopped into small 'pea-size' dice

Topping
1 cup brown sugar
100 grams butter
1 cup coconut
4 tablespoons milk

Combine chopped dates with baking soda and 1 cup boiling juice or cider. Set aside until cool, about 1 hour.

In a food processor mix butter and sugar until light and fluffy, add eggs and vanilla then flour. By hand, mix in dates, liquid and the chopped apple. Pour mix into a deep 20 cm tin, well-greased and with the base lined with baking paper. Bake at 180°C for 40–45 minutes until firm and the top looks set.

Stir topping ingredients in a small saucepan over medium heat until smooth and well combined.

Remove cake from oven, spoon topping over and cook 25–30 minutes or more at 180°C until topping is golden and cake cooked through. Cool in tin.

APRICOT ALMOND BISCOTTI

A new take on the Italian twice-baked crispy bickie, ideal for dunking in coffee or vino. These keep very well and look great wrapped in little cellophane bags for gifts.

3 cups flour
1 1/2 cups sugar
125 grams butter
2 teaspoons baking powder
1 teaspoon salt
1 teaspoon ground ginger
100 grams white chocolate, chopped (Milky Bar or white chocolate melts)
1 1/2 cups whole blanched almonds, toasted
2 eggs
1/2 cup orange or apricot flavoured liqueur (Cointreau or Apricot Brandy)
1 teaspoon almond essence
1 cup chopped dried apricots

Line a flat baking tray with non-stick baking paper or well-greased tinfoil. In a food processor combine flour, sugar, butter, baking powder, salt and ginger and process until a fine breadcrumb texture forms. Add white chocolate and process until finely chopped. Add toasted almonds and chop coarsely using the on/off pulse button. In a large bowl beat eggs, liqueur and almond essence, mix in the flour mixture and apricots and stir until it forms a moist dough.

Divide mixture into three and form into three long sausage-like logs and place across the tray. (Moisten your fingertips in water to shape the logs.) Refrigerate about 30 minutes until the dough is quite firm. Bake in a preheated 180°C oven for approximately 30-35 minutes until the logs are golden. Cool completely with the whole tray resting on a wire rack.

Transfer to a cutting board when completely cold and cut into thick toast width slices. A serrated bread knife works best for this job. Arrange the slices, cut sides down, on a baking sheet and bake in a low oven at 150°C about 15 minutes each side, 30 minutes total. Cool completely on a wire rack and store in airtight containers. These biscotti keep extremely well for at least two weeks and also freeze well.

TROPICAL PASSION CAKE

Banana, pineapple, passionfruit and hazelnuts with a ginger cream cheese icing

Makes 1 large 3-layer cake

3 cups flour
1 teaspoon baking soda
1/2 teaspoon salt
1/2 teaspoon ground ginger
3 eggs
225 gram can crushed pineapple in natural juice
1 cup sugar
1 cup oil
1 teaspoon vanilla essence
3 bananas, mashed with a fork
1/2 cup passionfruit pulp
1 cup toasted peeled hazelnuts, chopped

Ginger Icing
50 grams butter, softened
150 grams cream cheese, softened
1 1/2 cup icing sugar
1/2 teaspoon vanilla essence
10 pieces crystallised ginger, finely chopped

Preheat oven to 180°C (fan-bake is preferable). In a food processor mix eggs and sugar until pale creamy and smooth, add the oil, vanilla essence and bananas, then the flour, baking soda, salt and ginger. Add pineapple, passionfruit pulp and nuts and run machine just enough to mix in — do not over process these last 3 ingredients. Pour into a well-greased round cake tin 23–25cm and bake approximately 1 1/2 hours until risen and golden brown. Test that the cake is cooked through by inserting a skewer in the middle, which should come out clean. Cool in the tin for 1/2 hour then remove to a wire rack and cool completely. Frost when cold.

Ginger icing

Mix butter, cream cheese, vanilla essence and crystallised ginger in a food processor. Tip out into a medium-size bowl and beat in icing sugar with a wooden spoon until well combined. Split the cake into 3 layers and fill with cream cheese frosting then spread over the top and sides of cake. Leave to set before slicing to serve.

SPEEDY MICROWAVE MOIST CHOCOLATE CAKE

2 eggs
1 cup sugar
1 cup milk
1 cup oil (soya or canola)
3 tablespoons golden syrup
1 1/2 cups flour
3 heaped tablespoons cocoa
1 teaspoon baking powder
1 teaspoon baking soda

Mix all together in a food processor until smooth. Pour into a well-greased microwave ring cake tin and cook on high (850–900 watts) for 8–10 minutes. Cool in the tin, then serve with whipped cream and chocolate fudge sauce (see recipe on page 112).

CHOCOLATE PRUNE
& PORT TRUFFLES

Makes about 40

375 grams dark chocolate (1 packet chocolate melts)
200 grams butter
1/2 packet pitted prunes (about 20 prunes, I love the Sunsweet orange-flavoured ones)
1/4 cup port
3 cups icing sugar
2 extra packets dark chocolate melts, to dip truffles

Place chocolate and butter in a microwave-proof bowl and microwave cook on medium to high until melted, about 4 minutes, depending on microwave power levels. Stir a couple of times during cooking. Chop up prunes, checking there are no stones remaining and place in a small microwave-proof bowl with the port. Cook on high for 2–3 minutes to plump up. Mix the chocolate, butter, prunes and port together with the icing sugar until well combined. Chill in the fridge until firm enough to roll into generous small walnut-size balls. (The mixture is quite runny and soft when you first prepare it but should take 30 minutes to an hour to firm up in the fridge. If it goes too solid just microwave again on medium to soften to the right consistency.) Place the balls of mixture on a foil-lined tray and freeze until really solid, about 2 hours. Melt the 2 packets of chocolate melts on medium to low power stirring often, or over a bowl of hot water. If you're not familiar with microwave melting techniques, the instructions on the chocolate packet are very clear. Dip the frozen truffles in the melted chocolate. I find the small chocolate dipping fork made especially for this job quite invaluable. They are available from good cookware shops and are quite inexpensive. Drip off excess chocolate and allow to set on a tinfoil-covered tray. DO NOT store the finished truffles in the fridge as the chocolate tends to sweat — just keep them in a cool place. I usually have a plastic container filled with truffles which are prepared up to the dipping stage in the freezer at all times. It's very easy to quickly dip a few and you automatically have a treat ready to have with coffee or a small homemade gift or an alternative to a pud after a bigger meal.

Chocolate prune and port truffles

BABY PECAN PIES

Makes 16

These are an absolute favourite recipe of mine and great to have for dessert or as a treat with coffee, or as a biscuit foodie gift. They keep well in an airtight container.

125 grams butter
1 cup flour
1/2 cup icing sugar
1 cup pecans
60 grams butter, melted
1 egg
1 cup brown sugar
1 teaspoon vanilla essence

Place 125 grams butter, flour and icing sugar in a food processor and run machine until the pastry clumps together in a ball. Divide into 16 balls and with floured hands press the pastry into the bases and up the sides of non-stick (or well-greased) mini muffin tins. Refrigerate at least 30 minutes. Pastry will set quite firm, and you bake it cold like this. Divide the pecans between the chilled pastry cases, breaking the nuts as required. Mix melted butter, egg, brown sugar and vanilla until smooth and 'gluey' and spoon or pour carefully over the nuts. Do not overfill each little pie.

Bake in a preheated oven 180°C for 20–25 minutes until the pastry is golden brown and the filling puffed and crisp. Take out of the oven and leave in the mini muffin tins for a few minutes until they are cool enough to handle. Give each pie a little twist around to loosen the bottom and then carefully lift out to cool completely on a wire rack. They are delicious served warm and can be reheated easily and served with whipped cream or icecream.

Variations

Other nuts may be substituted for pecans. I have used walnuts, macadamias, almonds and hazelnuts all with great success and a mixture of nuts looks great for an alternative Christmas pudding. Finely chopped fresh apple, pear or apricot also works well with the butterscotch topping, but do not keep as long as nut filling.

LEMON CURD

Makes 3 x 250 gram jars.

Lemon curd can be used on toast and crumpets, as a filling for tarts or as icecream flavouring and with cakes such as the Greek coconut and lemon cake.

4 large juicy lemons
100 grams butter
2 cups sugar
4 eggs (beaten)

Scrub lemons then finely grate the rind and squeeze the juice. Place the juice and grated rind in a small saucepan. Add eggs, sugar and butter cut into little cubes. Stir over a very low heat until the sugar dissolves and then stir constantly for 2–3 minutes until the mixture thickens. Pour into a jug and then fill clean hot sterilised jars. Seal and keep refrigerated.

Variations
Replace 4 lemons with 6–8 juicy limes or 4 oranges or 1 cup passionfruit pulp.

'ONCE A YEAR' CHOCOLATE DIVINE DESSERT CAKE

Worth every calorie but no more often than 'once a year'. The texture is soft set chocolate mousse and, admit it, when was the last time you turned down a slice of chocolate mousse cake? There are few other foods that evoke the response that chocolate does. This is the dessert of choice!

150 ml water
450 grams sugar
450 grams chocolate melts
450 grams butter
6 eggs
1 cup flour
whipped cream, to serve

Line the base of two 23 cm springform cake tins with non-stick baking paper. Place sugar and water in a medium saucepan and stir over gentle heat until sugar dissolves. Bring to the boil and boil for 1 minute. Add the chocolate and butter to the saucepan, stir until melted and remove from heat. Whisk eggs in the food processor, add flour and mix well. Add the chocolate mixture and mix until well combined, then pour into the 2 prepared tins. Place tins in a large roasting pan and fill pan with enough water to come halfway up the sides of the springform tins. Bake in a preheated oven 180°C for 45–55 minutes, topping up the water if it evaporates. The cakes should be firm to the touch in the centre. Leave cakes for an hour in the tin to cool and then tip out onto a greaseproof paper-covered wire rack.

When cold, wrap in plastic wrap and refrigerate overnight. Put cakes together with whipped cream and dust top with icing sugar and cocoa. This cake looks really fabulous with strawberries piled over and around it.

INDEX